The Language of
Visual Effects

To my former mentor
DENNIS MUREN

The Language of Visual Effects

MICHEAL J. MCALISTER

Lone Eagle Publishing Company
Los Angeles, California

THE LANGUAGE OF VISUAL EFFECTS

LONE EAGLE PUBLISHING CO.
2337 Roscomare Road, Suite Nine
Los Angeles, CA 90077-1851
310/471-8066 • FAX 310/471-4969

Printed in the United States of America

Photos on the following pages courtesy of Lucasfilm Ltd:
7, 74, 79, 87, 89, 90, 91, 94, 95, 99, 105, 110, 124, 125, 138, 150, 151

Photo on page 5 courtesy of Mechanical Concepts.

Photo on page 38 courtesy of Paramount Pictures.

Illustrations on pages 92-93 (Hue Circle; Subtractive Colors; Additive Colors) by Andy Markley—Art 101, Roseville, California

Cover design by Heidi Frieder

Library of Congress Cataloging-in-Publication Data

McAlister, Micheal, 1954-
The language of visual effects / Micheal McAlister
p. cm.
Includes index.
ISBN 0-943728-47-9 (paper only)
1. Cinematography—Special effects—Dictionaries.
TR858.M325 1992
778.5'345'03—dc20 92-16846
CIP

INTRODUCTION

"ROTOSCOPE?"
"What is ROTOSCOPE?"
"Would you explain ROTOSCOPE?"
"What on earth do you mean, ROTOSCOPE?"

Eleven years of this sort of questioning would convince just about anyone of the need for a concise glossary of visual effects terminology. As is so often the case with specialized fields, the language which shrouds the visual effects arena is unyielding and intimidating. Conversations with highly intelligent men and women have been known to come to a grinding halt at the mere mention of the words "ARTICULATE MATTE." I know. I've seen it happen.

THE LANGUAGE OF VISUAL EFFECTS is meant to be used as a dictionary/encyclopedia by working professionals and students alike. Keep it handy on the bookshelf or in your back pocket for those moments when effects people lose their heads and speak gibberish (it happens to them all.) Keep it at your side while reading the "how to" write-ups following each major effects film release. But most important of all, keep those visual effects conversations understood.

Nothing would please me more than to find this glossary helpful to the thousands of busy professional filmmakers who barely have time to talk on the telephone, let alone study. The concise definitions and brief discussions within this book should give the reader adequate knowledge to stay focused and informed during conversations that involve even more than one effects person at a time.

This book is not a history of visual effects. It is not a "how to do it" book. I refer readers interested in detailed discussions of the topics herein to the many other books on the subject. To the rest of you, please enjoy!

The entries within this book have been selected, more or less, on the basis of whether or not I have ever heard of the term. At the risk of sounding arrogant, I figured that if I did not need to know the meaning of the word during my eleven years around the top of the visual effects pyramid, then you certainly don't need to know the meaning now. Why waste your time and my printer ribbon?

Before getting to the thank you portion of this introduction I wish to offer a few pointers on having conversations with effects people:

1) CAST YOUR CONVERSATION

   Never attempt a conversation with an effects person who has more than one pen sticking out of his shirt pocket.

2) APPEAL TO THEIR SYMPATHY

   If at all possible, look as stupid as a doorknob when first meeting them. (A glassed-over gaze while delivering a crushing handshake is an effective touch.)

3) THREATEN THEM

   If all else fails, do not give them the job until they speak English to you. Somewhere in the ancient history of their education is infantile babbling, which at times is much more intelligible to an outsider than conversations they have among themselves.

So much for the friends I used to have in the effects business.

To the friends who helped me with this book, I offer my sincere gratitude. Dan Kolsrud gave me the idea. Cheryl Nardi, my best friend, actually read the entire first draft cover to cover. Les Dittert, Steve Wright, John Lassiter, Tom Porter, Ralph Guggenheim, and George Joblov helped clear the fog in my mind regarding the ever-changing fields of digital effects and computer graphics. Thanks to Don Shay of that fine magazine, Cinefex, for his endorsement and comments. Thanks to Tom Joyner, Jim Herbert, and George Lucas for their endorsements as well. Thanks for encouragement from Ralph Winter and Paul Haggar. Thanks to Charles Champlin for introducing me to Lone Eagle, and Joan Singleton, my publisher and editor (I love the way that sounds), who improved the book with her comments on the first draft. Thanks to my wife, Gilliane, who gave birth to my daughter Dominique, who in turn was the reason I stuck around the house long enough to finish this book. And finally to my friends at Industrial Light and Magic. Thanks for all you have taught me, not only about visual effects, but about teamwork, professionalism, artistry and pride.

Mike

Mike McAlister

ABBEY
Nickname for ABEKAS.

ABEKAS™
A DIGITAL video disc recorder capable of SINGLE FRAME record and playback. The Abekas can store several seconds of video information and is therefore useful as a slow motion or real time playback system for COMPUTER GENERATED IMAGERY.

ACADEMY APERTURE
The standard aperture for 35 mm motion pictures. The image area is positioned to the right of center on the NEGATIVE thus allowing for a strip of about one–tenth of an inch for the sound track.
(See FRAME illustration on page 55.)

ACETATE BASE
A relatively fire resistant and chemically stable film base upon which an EMULSION is then placed. Acetate based films are infinitely safer and age better than their highly combustible nitrate based predecessors. Most visual effects processes use acetate based film stocks, but often the stronger ESTAR based film stocks are required.

ADDITIVE COLOR PRINTER
A printer which mixes each of the three ADDITIVE PRIMARY COLORS of light onto a single piece of film to yield a color balanced scene.

ADDITIVE COLORS
See ADDITIVE PRIMARY COLORS.

ADDITIVE PRIMARY COLORS
In photography, the colors red, green and blue, of which all other colors are combinations. When light of these colors is mixed together in equal measures, WHITE LIGHT is the result. These primary colors play a critical role in various

photographic processes, including the BLUESCREEN PROCESS. See COLOR TRIANGLE and SUBTRACTIVE PRIMARY COLORS.
(See illustration on page 92.)

ADDRESS
The exact location in computer memory where a particular piece of data is stored.

AERIAL IMAGE
A projected image which is focused onto a plane in mid–air. Since the image is not focused onto an object such as a movie screen, it is not visible to the naked eye. However, the image is quite real and could be seen by simply holding a piece of white paper at the plane of focus. If such an experiment were to be conducted, the image seen against the piece of paper would be called a VIRTUAL IMAGE. Once the paper is removed the now–invisible image still exists, but only as an "aerial image." Thus an aerial image is in contrast with a VIRTUAL IMAGE.

AERIAL–IMAGE PRINTER
The backbone of OPTICAL COMPOSITE PHOTOGRAPHY. A printer of this type projects an image into the lens of a TAKING CAMERA. The projected image, which is not visible to the naked eye, is focused onto a plane in mid–air between the projector and camera lenses, hence the name "Aerial–Image Printer." The lens of the taking camera then captures this mid–air image and focuses it onto the film plane.

AERIAL PERSPECTIVE
The natural effect in which successively more distant objects appear less distinct to the eye. In miniature photography and other visual effects techniques aerial perspective becomes of critical importance. Objects in the distance of a scene should have less color saturation and appear fuzzier than those in the foreground.
(See illustration on page 89.)

AIRBRUSH
A very small paint spraying device used by artists to create paintings with very soft images or graduated tonal or color scales. Airbrushes are held and used in much the same manner as a normal brush and have a similar effect as

painting with a tiny spray paint can. In computer and VIDEO PAINTBOX SYSTEMS an "airbrush style" pen can be selected for painting or altering of the image.

ALGORITHM
A strategy or set of instructions for solving a computing problem by issuing a series of step by step computer programming commands. An algorithm is independent of the actual programming language to be used, and can be thought of as the "recipe" a "computer programming cook" uses to achieve a result.

ALIASING
The jagged lines visible in lower resolution forms of COMPUTER GRAPHICS caused by inadequate electronic filtering. Also known as JAGGIES, aliasing causes a diagonal line to appear as a "STAIRSTEP" instead of a smooth line. ANTIALIASING refers to various techniques employed to eliminate this problem.

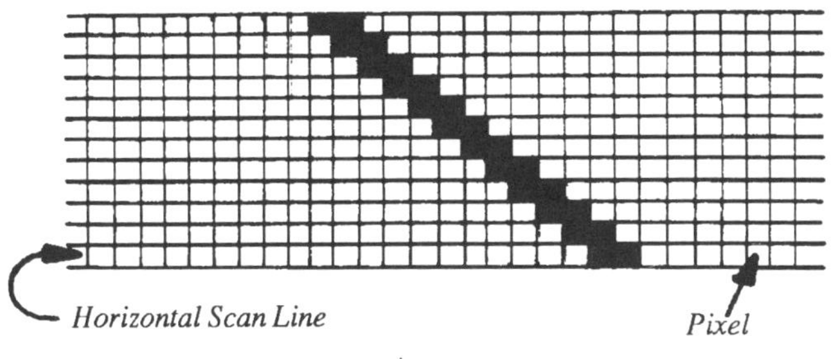

ALIASING

ALPHA CHANNEL
A computer stores PICTURE ELEMENTS or PIXELS, in four distinct pieces or CHANNELS. Channels One, Two and Three contain the image components of red, green and blue colors. Channel Four is called the "alpha channel" and is often used to carry additional information about the eventual compositing of the image. Such information might include the degree of transparency of the image as defined by the density of the associated MATTE.

ALPHANUMERIC
Computer data that consists of numbers or letters.

ANALOG
An electronic signal composed of varying voltage levels. Analog signals are of much lower quality than the newer DIGITAL signals, and are subject to serious DEGRADATION when duplicated.

ANAMORPHIC LENS
Refers to any lens which compresses the horizontal axis of a scene to ultimately yield a widescreen exhibition format. The most common anamorphic projection ASPECT RATIO is that of panavision, 2.35:1.

ANAMORPHIC FORMAT
Any film format in which the image is squeezed along a horizontal axis during photography and unsqueezed during projection. The result is a wider than normal picture ASPECT RATIO.

ANIMATED ON ONES/TWOS
See ON ONES/TWOS.

ANIMATED WIPE
See REVEAL MATTE.

ANIMATIC
A rough simulation of a particular scene which is achieved by photographing storyboards or drawings which illustrate the critical action and timing of that scene. See VIDEOMATIC.

ANIMATION
The process of photographing drawings, puppets, or inanimate objects one FRAME at a time to yield the illusion of movement. Incremental changes in position, form or appearance between frame EXPOSURES provides this illusion when the resultant film is projected at normal film rates. Animation techniques come to bear on a multitude of visual effects challenges.

ANIMATION CAMERA
A special camera designed specifically to shoot in SINGLE FRAME or slow motion modes. The camera is typically mounted on a vertical column above a flat table upon which the artwork is placed. The camera moves up and down along the column to alter the field of view while the table is capable of moving right and left (east or west) and up or down (north

or south) to create very complex moves. Most tables can also rotate on a horizontal plane. Almost all animation cameras used in visual effects today are linked to a MOTION CONTROL SYSTEM of some type. The combination of camera, vertical column, and table are commonly referred to as an ANIMATION STAND or ROSTRUM CAMERA.

ANIMATION CAMERA

Animation Camera manufactured by Mechanical Concepts. Photo courtesy Mechanical Concepts, Inc.

ANIMATION CELS
Clear sheets of acetate onto which a multitude of images is placed for the purpose of filming under an animation camera.

ANIMATION CYCLE
Any particular group of animation drawings which completes a specific action. Typically an animation cycle could be photographed several times back–to–back to complete a repetitive version of the action, such as a man walking or a dog chasing its tail.

ANIMATION STAND
See ANIMATION CAMERA.

ANIMATOR
The individual who creates the drawings or otherwise manipulates artwork for an animated effect. See also STOP MOTION ANIMATOR.

ANIMATRONIC
Generally refers to any creature or puppet likeness of human or animal whose movements are controlled through the use of electronic, mechanical or radio control devices.

ANSWER PRINT
The first print a lab produces of a finished film which attempts correct color for all scenes. The "first answer" print is followed by the "second answer" and "third answer" etc, until all scenes are correct.

ANTIALIASING
See ALIASING.

APERTURE
1) The opening in the movement of a camera which determines the area of the film to be exposed.
2) The opening in the diaphragm of a lens which allows light to pass through.

APPLICATION
A task to be completed by a computer program. Applications range from common word processing programs to complicated PAINT SYSTEMS and COMPUTER ANIMATION SYSTEMS.

ARCHITECTURE
The overall structure of computer SOFTWARE and HARDWARE in terms of how the two interact.

ARMATURE
The skeletal insides of a stop motion puppet which are generally constructed of chrome plated ball and socket joints with machined steel "bones."

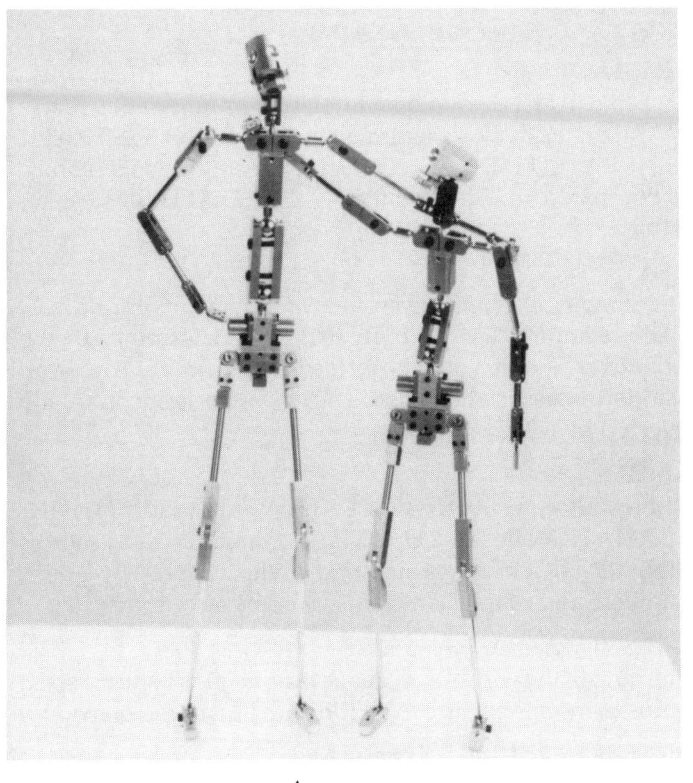

ARMATURES
Armatures for use inside a Stop Motion puppet. Photo courtesy Lucasfilm Ltd.

ARMATURE WIRE
Aluminum wire of various gauges which is commonly used as a skeletal support for large clay sculptures. Armature wire is occasionally used as the sole ARMATURE in a stop motion puppet in applications where the animation is quite simple.

ARTIC MATTE
See ARTICULATE MATTE.

ARTICULATE MATTE
Any MATTE which is hand drawn frame–by–frame to conform to a moving image. Articulate mattes are normally created on a ROTOSCOPE STAND and are used to prevent a background object from double–exposing over a foreground ELEMENT or vice versa. See BLUESCREEN PROCESS.
(See ROTOSCOPE illustration on page 124.)

ARTIFACT
A visible defect caused by a limitation or bug in the SOFTWARE or mechanical equipment used to make COMPUTER GENERATED IMAGES. Artifacts are continuous in nature as compared to a momentary GLITCH. ALIASING is an artifact.

ASA
The numerical rating given to any particular film EMULSION relating to its sensitivity to light as determined by the American National Standards Institute (formerly American Standards Association, hence ASA.) Also less commonly referred to as ISO or DIN.

ASCII
Abbreviation for AMERICAN STANDARD CODE OF INFORMATION INTERCHANGE. A commonly used code of BINARY DIGITS (ones and zeros) which represent letters, numbers and other characters for use by a computer.

ASPECT RATIO
The ratio of the width of an image to its height. Typical aspect ratios in motion picture exhibition are illustrated on page 9.

ATMOSPHERIC PERSPECTIVE
See AERIAL PERSPECTIVE.

ATTRIBUTE
Computer terminology which refers to the visual characteristics of an image, such as the color and value of the image. In word processing programs attributes include the size and appearance of typeface, such as boldface, italics, etc.

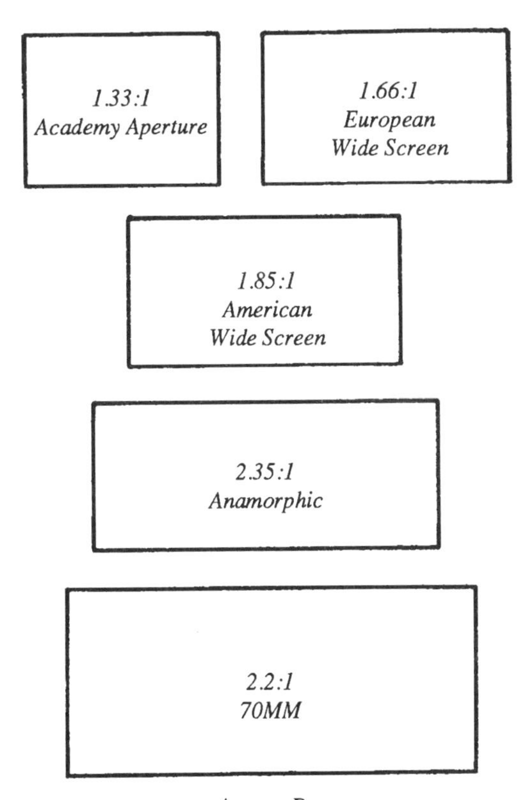

ASPECT RATIO

AUTOFOCUS
An electro–mechanical device which automatically maintains focus at a predetermined plane as the camera distance from that plane changes. Autofocus devices are essential on animation cameras and very handy on MOTION CONTROL TRACK CAMERAS and OPTICAL PRINTERS.

AUTOMATTE CAMERA
A computer controlled multi–plane camera designed by Industrial Light and Magic company which is used to photograph MATTE PAINTINGs and small miniature sets.

AUXILIARY STORAGE
Computer memory storage devices such as DISC DRIVES or MAGNETIC TAPE devices which store massive amounts of data beyond the computer's internal storage capacity.

AXIS
The imaginary line around which an object rotates.

BACK AND FORTH PRINTING
The printing of a certain number of frames of film first forward, for example from one to ten, then in reverse from ten to one. This can be repeated endlessly to obtain a recurring cycle of action such as the swinging of a pendulum or the rocking of a chair.

BACKGROUND
In COMPOSITES of several layers, the BACKGROUND ELEMENT is the one over which all others are matted. BACKGROUND images generally comprise the majority of the composition.

BACKGROUND PLATE
Common name given to the image to be used in the BACKGROUND of a COMPOSITE scene. The term "plate" is a throwback to the era when BACKGROUNDs were actually filmed as still photographs on glass plates. Frequently BACKGROUND plates are referred to as simply "PLATES" in the context of their filming. For instance a "plate shoot" would refer to the filming of a BACKGROUND ELEMENT for a particular scene.

BACKGROUND PROJECTION
See FRONT PROJECTION and REAR PROJECTION.

BACKING
A backdrop, often painted with elaborate scenery, used in conjunction with a foreground set. See CYCLORAMA.
(See BACKING photograph on page 89.)

BACK–LIT ANIMATION
See BOTTOM–LIT ANIMATION.

BACK PROJECTION
See REAR PROJECTION.

BASE
The clear cellulose acetate or polyester film which serves as the carrier of the EMULSION of any film stock. See ACETATE BASE and ESTAR BASE.

BAUD RATE
The rate at which DIGITAL information can be exchanged between computer based equipment. The baud rates of equipment used to create and store DIGITAL IMAGES becomes critical due to the massive amounts of data required to make a HIGH RESOLUTION picture.

BC
Abbreviation for BLACK CENTER MATTE. See MALE MATTE.

BEADED SCREEN
A highly reflective screen composed of microscopic beads of glass used in the process of FRONT PROJECTION. A screen of this sort manufactured by 3–M carries the trademarked name Scotchlite. See FRONT PROJECTION SCREEN.

BEAM SPLITTER
See FIFTY–FIFTY MIRROR.

BEAUTY PASS
In MULTIPLE PASS PHOTOGRAPHY, the PASS which provides most of the significant detail and lighting scheme of a subject. See PASS.

BELL AND HOWELL PERFORATION
Also called NEGATIVE PERFORATIONS, the rectangular sprocket holes with curved sides which are largely standard on all 35 mm NEGATIVE and duplication film stocks. They are favored over KODAK STANDARD PERFORATIONS for use on negative film stocks due to their steadier REGISTRATION.
(See PERFORATION illustration on page 108.)

BELLOWS
A rubber air bladder or balloon which is inserted into prosthetic makeups or rubber creatures to create a "breathing" movement when the bladder is inflated and deflated.

BELLOWS ATTACHMENT
An accordion–like chamber which mounts between the faceplate of a camera and the rear of a lens in order to maintain

a tunnel of darkness as the lens is moved away from the camera during closeup focusing.

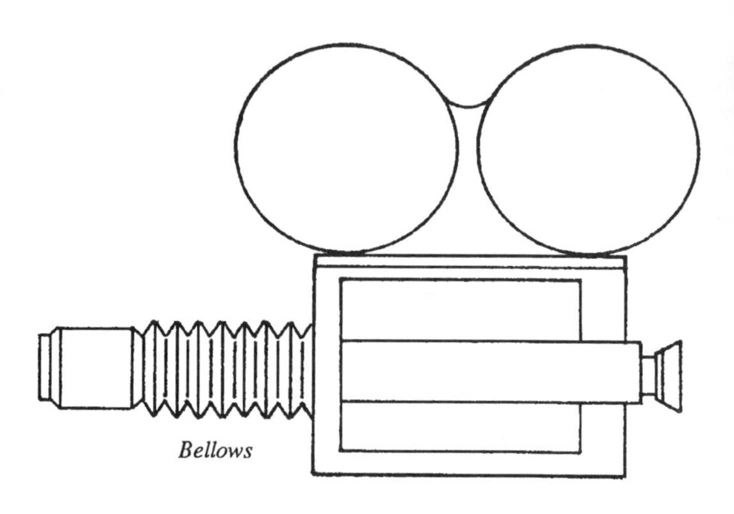

BELLOWS ATTACHMENT

BG
Abbreviation for BACKGROUND.

BIG PIN
See PILOT PIN and REGISTRATION PINS.

BINARY
A numbering system based on the digits 1 and 0. All computer data is stored in binary form. A value of 1 is the equivalent of a "yes" or "on" decision, while a value of 0 is the equivalent of a "no" or "off" decision.

BINARY DIGIT
See BIT.

BIPACK
The process of simultaneously passing two separate pieces of film through any camera, printer or projection system.

BIPACK CAMERA
A camera which has been dedicated for use in any BIPACK operation. Special adjustments frequently must be made to allow the two pieces of film to pass through the FILM GATE while maintaining STEADINESS.

BIPACK MAGAZINE
A light–proof chamber attached to a camera which has been specially designed to simultaneously hold two rolls of film both before and after EXPOSURE.
(See illustration below.)

BIPACK PRINTER
See CONTACT PRINTER.

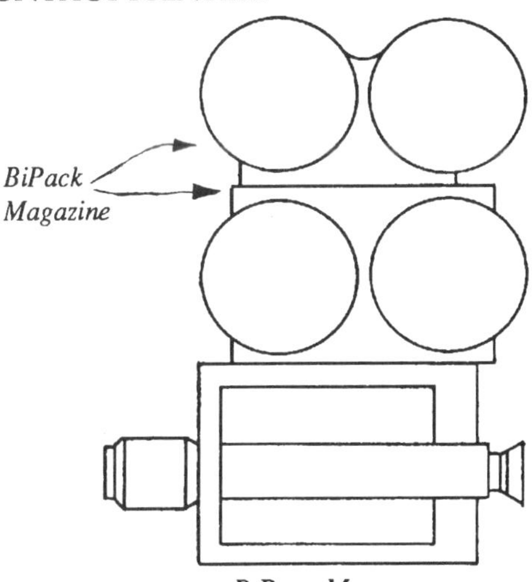

BiPack Magazine

BIPACK PRINTING
A process which utilizes a BIPACK CAMERA to combine two or more separate film images onto one piece of film. The first piece of film containing a developed image is loaded into the forward position in the camera FILM GATE, with a fresh piece of film stock sandwiched behind. The camera is then focused on a white card which is partially painted black. Light from the white portion of the card passes through the lens, through the developed image, and onto the raw stock behind. The black portion of the card prevents the rest of the developed image from printing. The RAWSTOCK is re-wound and a second piece of film containing a developed image replaces the first. The black and white areas of the card are reversed and the printing pass is repeated. This time the previously exposed area of the rawstock is protected by the black area of the card, while the unexposed portion of the NEGATIVE receives the second image. This process can be

used to combine any number of different types of images, from live action to MATTE PAINTINGs and miniatures.
(See illustration below)

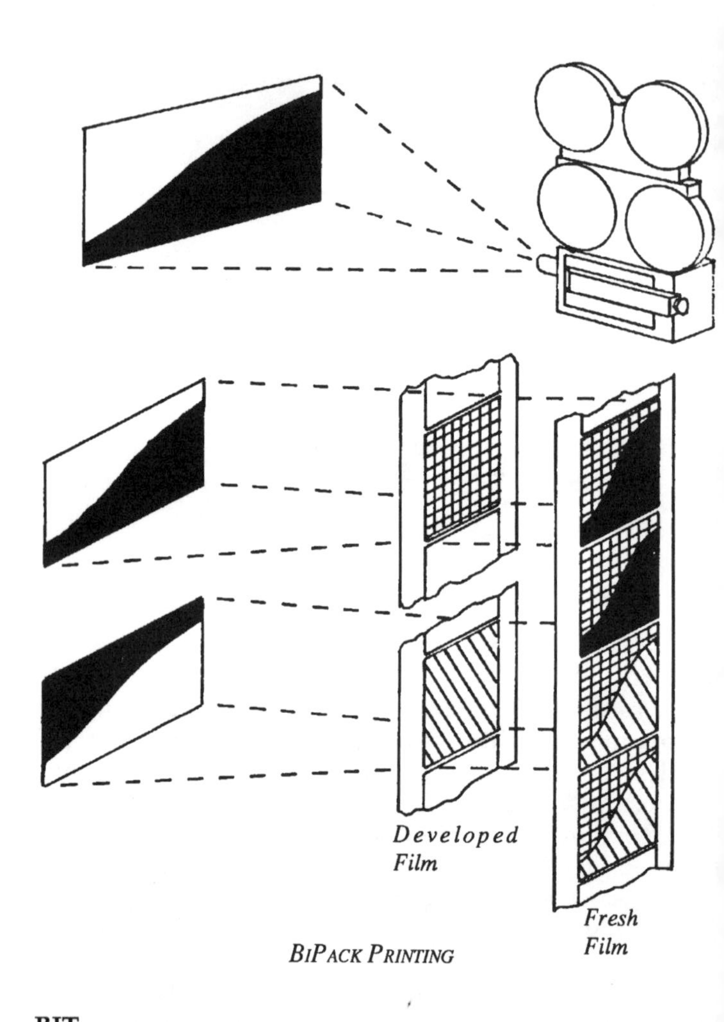

BIPACK PRINTING

BIT
Abbreviation for BINARY DIGIT. The basic unit of information that is the foundation of all computing. It is the electronic equivalent of an on/off, yes/no decision.

BITMAP GRAPHICS
A COMPUTER GRAPHICS term which refers to an image which is created by assigning distinct color and brightness information to each PIXEL of the image. Bitmap graphics offer absolute control over the image up to the limit of resolution and are the makeup of high end COMPUTER GRAPHICS systems. See also OBJECT–ORIENTED GRAPHICS.

BLACK AND WHITE DUPE
A black and white copy of an edited sequence showing the context within a movie of the various effects shots to be produced.

BLACK CENTER MATTE
See MALE MATTE.

BLACK CORE MATTE
See MALE MATTE.

BLACKSCREEN
A pure black BACKING often used to photograph objects in LIMBO for eventual MATTING or DOUBLE EXPOSURE into a scene.

BLEED THROUGH
See PRINT THROUGH.

BLEND LINE
The area at which two separate images join to create a single COMPOSITE. The two images are "blended" into one another. This term refers primarily to MATTE PAINTINGS and SPLIT SCREEN effects.

BLIMP
A sound dampening case into which noisy cameras are placed while filming dialogue sequences. The camera "looks" through a window at the front of the blimp and is operated from the outside.

BLOOP LIGHT
An electronic method of marking film in a TAKING CAMERA with a FLASH FRAME as a shot is being filmed. This system is useful (if not essential) when shooting LIVE ACTION MOTION CONTROL shots in which two or more ELEMENTS with the same camera move must be synchronized for COMPOSITE. In this application the "bloop light" is triggered by the same

computer which is controlling the movement of the camera, thus ensuring that the flash frame appears on exactly the same frame relative to the camera's action during each take.

BLOW UP
The process of enlarging a film image, usually while making a duplicate on an OPTICAL PRINTER.

BLUE BACKING
See BLUESCREEN.

BLUE MAX™
Specialized FRONT PROJECTION BLUESCREEN equipment developed by APOGEE, INC., to address the problem of obtaining high quality bluescreen images of reflective subjects.

BLUE PRINT
A black and white image made by shining blue light through the NEGATIVE of a BLUESCREEN image. The blue print is then used to help generate the various MATTES required for a bluescreen COMPOSITE. See BLUESCREEN PROCESS.

BLUE RECORD
See COLOR SEPARATIONS.

BLUESCREEN
A large primary blue backing against which a subject is photographed in LIMBO. Bluescreens may either be front lit or back lit but in either case the color of blue must be devoid of any red or green pigments in order to expose only the blue layer of a film EMULSION. The most common type of bluescreen is called a "STEWART T–MATTE" blue screen. This is a sheet of transparent and flexible blue plastic which is stretched between a rigid frame and lit from behind.
(See BLUESCRENN photographs on pages 90-91.)

BLUESCREEN PADDLE
Rigid plastic "wands" ranging in width and length from one to thirty–six inches or more and constructed of neon tubes covered by translucent plastic the color of bluescreens. Paddles can be mounted in various configurations or hand held as the specific shot requires to cover mounting rods or equipment which might otherwise intrude behind the silhouette of the subject being isolated against the bluescreen. Use of a bluescreen paddle eliminates the need for an ARTICULATE MATTE to isolate the subject from its surroundings.

BLUESCREEN PLATE
A bluescreen shot involving actors is generally referred to as a bluescreen plate.

BLUESCREEN PROCESS
A very popular TRAVELING MATTE process which involves the photography of a subject isolated against a field of primary blue. Through a series of complicated steps on an OPTICAL PRINTER the blue portion of the image is extracted and treated in various ways to generate MALE and FEMALE MATTES. These mattes are then used to COMPOSITE the original bluescreen subject into a BACKGROUND.
(See BLUESCREEN photographs on pages 90-91.)

BLUE SPILL
The contamination of the foreground subject with blue light emanating from the BLUESCREEN. This "spilled blue light," which looks like a blue reflection on the subject, creates holes in the mattes made from the resultant image. It is safe to say that a major portion of any bluescreen shoot is absorbed dealing with this problem. An alternative to dealing with the blue spill on the set would be to hand draw BLUE SPILL MATTES.

BLUE SPILL MATTE
A MATTE which is hand drawn under a ROTOSCOPE STAND to isolate an area of a BLUESCREEN subject which has been contaminated by BLUE SPILL. This is a very labor intensive process which must be performed with the greatest skill. This new matte in many cases conforms to the edge of the foreground and therefore must fit perfectly to avoid a MATTE line. See BLUESCREEN PROCESS.

BOOT
The computer term for turning on a computer system or loading a program into the computer.

BOTTOM LIT ANIMATION
Animation which uses a light source positioned behind the artwork. This technique utilizes KODALITH transparencies, and other types of transparent or translucent artwork. Also called BACKLIT ANIMATION.

BRACKETING
See EXPOSURE WEDGE.

BREAKDOWN
A written analysis of the needs of a script, in this case the visual effects including scene descriptions and approaches to be taken in their creation. In most cases a breakdown must be made before a meaningful budget can be determined.

BS
Abbreviation for BLUESCREEN.

B–SPLINE
A COMPUTER GRAPHICS technique for approximating a complex curved surface by using a relatively small number of key points interconnected by a series of straight lines.

BUCKLE SWITCH
A switch inside a camera or FILM MAGAZINE which prevents damage to the camera or piece of NEGATIVE by immediately shutting down camera power should a film jam occur.

BUFFER
Temporary storage area within a computer or an external device such as an OPTICAL DISC used to hold data until it is required for processing.

BUG
A defect in either computer SOFTWARE or HARDWARE. The term originates from the presence of a short–circuit inducing insect which wandered into the vacuum tube circuitry of the first electronic hardware.

BULLET PROOF MATTE
A nickname given to a MATTE with density so great that no light is transmitted at all.

BUMP MAPPING
A technique in COMPUTER GRAPHICS in which an object is given a surface roughness or bumpiness of infinite variety. For example, a cobblestone texture could be applied to a concrete driveway using a bump map.

BURN IN
A process in which a shot ELEMENT is simply double exposed ("burned in") over existing imagery rather than being matted.

BURN IN MATTE
See FEMALE MATTE.

BUS
An electronic circuit, roughly analogous to a city freeway, which serves as a pathway through which information is exchanged within or between computers and other devices.

BUTTERFLY CAMERA
A light weight but noisy VISTAVISION camera convenient for use in aerial photography and other M.O.S. applications.

BYTE
The amount of computer memory required to store a single character. A byte contains eight BITS of information, and is the smallest addressable unit of data.

C

CAMERA JACK
A device used to securely lock–off a tripod head in order to hold a camera perfectly still while shooting a MATTE SHOT.

CAMERA MOVEMENT
The portion of a motion picture camera which transports and positions the film in preparation for exposure. Critical components of a camera movement include the APERTURE, FILM GATE, REGISTRATION PINS, PULL DOWN CLAW, and various sprocket wheels and film guides.
(See illustration on page 20.)

CAMERA ORIGINAL
The piece of NEGATIVE film onto which a scene is first exposed. Also called ORIGINAL NEGATIVE.

CAPPING SHUTTER
A secondary shutter positioned between the lens and the primary shutter of an animation or MOTION CONTROL CAMERA. The capping shutter prevents light from striking the film between EXPOSURES.

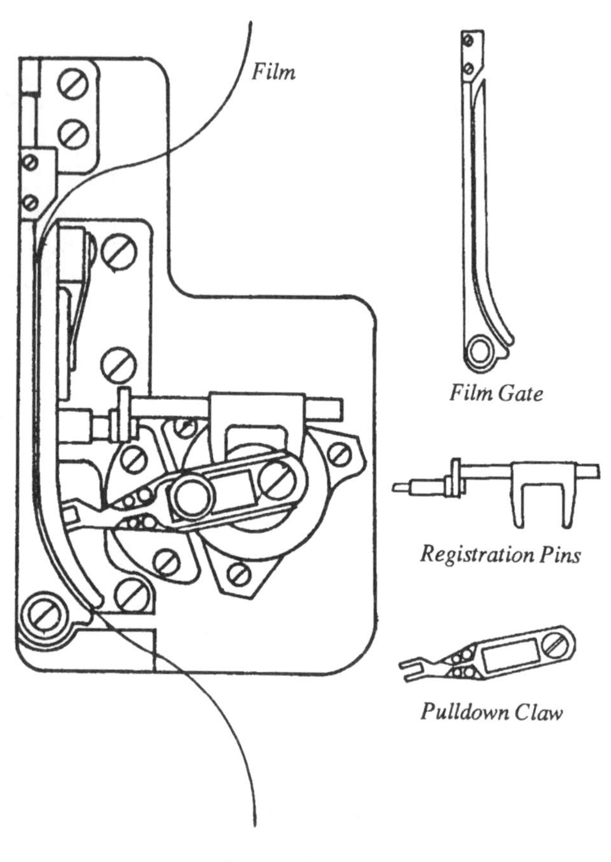

CAMERA MOVEMENT

CATHODE RAY TUBE
A television or video MONITOR picture tube. The abbreviation, CRT, is common jargon referring to any video monitor.

CCD
Abbreviation for CHARGED COUPLED DEVICE. A light sensitive electronic chip used as a temporary image storage device for INPUT SCANNERS and video cameras. When light strikes a CCD, the color and brightness information is converted to a small array of binary digits which are meaningful to the computer.

CCD ARRAY
A two dimensional assembly of CCD chips arranged into rows and columns and used as an image recording device for video cameras and high resolution film INPUT SCANNERS.

CC FILTER
See COLOR CORRECTING FILTER.

CD–ROM COMPACT DISC – READ ONLY MEMORY
A type of OPTICAL DISC which is used to store massive amounts of data. The information is stored as a series of microscopic plateaus and valleys etched into the surface of the disc. Laser light reflecting off the surfaces of these plateaus is converted via electrical pulses into BINARY DATA.

CEL
See ANIMATION CELS.

CEL ANIMATION
Animation which uses as artwork a series of drawings made on clear acetate CELs. This term most often refers to cartoon type animation.

CELL
See ANIMATION CELS.

CEL PUNCH
A device used to punch REGISTER PEG holes into ANIMATION CELS or paper.

CENTRAL PROCESSING UNIT
Abbreviated CPU, the brain of a computer which interprets the SOFTWARE commands and executes the program.

CGI
Abbreviation for COMPUTER GENERATED IMAGERY.

CHANNEL
A MOTION CONTROL computer stores motion information for many axes of camera and model movement. Each AXIS of movement is called a "channel" and is given separate computer memory space. In COMPUTER GRAPHICS, channel refers to each of the red, green, blue and ALPHA components which together describe the color, brightness and degree of TRANSPARENCY of a single PIXEL.

CHARACTERISTIC CURVE
A plotted curve which illustrates the change in density of a NEGATIVE as the exposure is increased. The slope of this curve is the measure of GAMMA, or CONTRAST of a particular film stock. The curve is useful in predicting how a film stock will respond to various exposure conditions.

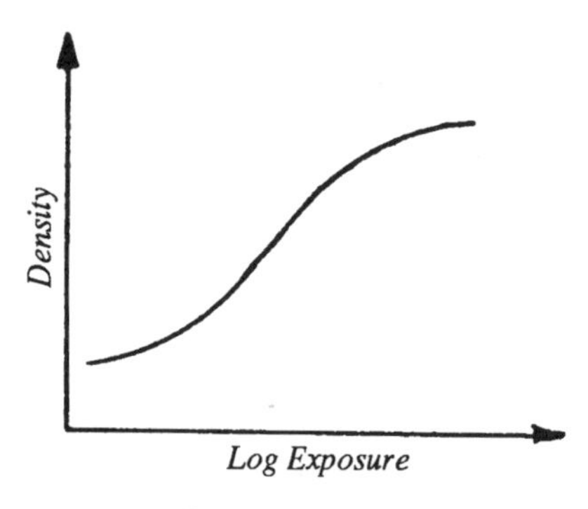

CHARACTERISTIC CURVE

CHARGED COUPLED DEVICE
See CCD.

CHATTER
The rhythmic movement between a foreground ELEMENT and its MATTE which appears on screen as a "fluttering" or "chatter" around the edges of the element. This is usually caused by UNSTEADINESS in any of the camera or projector movements used while making the various INTERMEDIATE COMPOSITING ELEMENTS.

CHEWING
A condition similar to CHATTER but originating from an improperly drawn ARTICULATE MATTE. At times while rotoscoping a blurred image the artist must "guess" where the actual edge of the image appears. If this guess is inconsistent from frame to frame, a "chewing" or "flutter" along the edge of the image will appear in the COMPOSITE.

CHIP
See COMPUTER CHIP.

CHIP CHART
A nickname for a standard COLOR SCALE used in conjunction with a grey scale. If a scene is COLOR TIMED correctly, the multiple colors on this chart will appear on screen exactly as they do to the naked eye. The term "chip" is derived from the small color squares which make up the chart.

CHROMA
The intensity of color in an image.

CHROMAKEYING
A video COLOR DIFFERENCE MATTING process similar in concept to the BLUESCREEN PROCESS. Used often to create special effects in video, chromakeying accomplishes the MATTING of images over one another in REAL TIME.

CINCH MARKS
Tiny scratches appearing on a piece of film caused by the surfaces of the film sliding over each other as a loose roll of film is tightened by pulling on one end.

CIRCUIT BOARD
A thin non–conductive panel onto which various electrical components are mounted and interconnected. Computers are typically made of one or more circuit boards which communicate with each other via a BUS.

CLAPBOARD
See CLAPSTICKS.

CLAPSTICKS
The familiar device used to make an audible and visible 'clap' on a piece of film and audio tape to facilitate syncing of the two at a later date.
(See illustration on page 24.)

CLAY ANIMATION™
The technique of STOP MOTION ANIMATION in which clay is sculpted and resculpted for each frame of a shot. The famous "California Raisins" are clay animation characters.

CLAYMATION
A trademarked name belonging to Will Vinton productions referring to the technique of CLAY ANIMATION.

CLEAR CENTER MATTE
See FEMALE MATTE.

CLAPSTICKS

CLEAR CORE MATTE
See FEMALE MATTE.

CLIP
A small piece of film cut or "clipped" from a scene for reference use.

CLOSEUP LENS
See DIOPTER LENS.

CLOUD TANK
A large aquarium–like tank of water used to film cloud effects and underwater miniatures.

CODE
The language which is used to issue instructions to a computer. MACHINE CODE is the set of BINARY DIGITS which is directly understood by a computer, whereas SOURCE CODE refers to the actual words and symbols as written in a programming language before it is interpreted by a computer.

COLLIMATOR
A device used to test photographic lenses for a variety of conditions, such as sharpness and focus distance accuracy.

COLOR BALANCE
A quality of a COMPOSITED scene in which all ELEMENTS within that scene appear to be their proper color relative to each other.

COLOR BARS
A set of electronically generated colors placed at the head of a video tape recording and used to initialize the color adjustment settings on electronic equipment. The video equivalent of a CHIP CHART.

COLOR CHART
See CHIP CHART.

COLOR COMPENSATING FILTER
See COLOR CORRECTING FILTER.

COLOR CORRECT
See COLOR TIMING.

COLOR CORRECTING FILTER
Small gelatin based color filters of incremented intensity used to make minor color corrections during photography or OPTICAL COMPOSITING. The colors most commonly used are red, green, blue, cyan, yellow and magenta.

COLOR DEPTH
The number of colors available for RENDERING COMPUTER GENERATED IMAGERY as determined by the number of BITS allotted to the storage of each PIXEL. The greater the number of bits, the greater the selection of color. Color depth is expressed as 8 BIT COLOR, 16 BIT COLOR, 24 BIT COLOR or 32 BIT COLOR.

COLOR DIFFERENCE MATTE PROCESS
See COLOR DIFFERENCE TRAVELING MATTE PROCESS.

COLOR DIFFERENCE TRAVELING MATTE PROCESS
Any of the MATTING processes which use color of the image as the basis for separating the desired image from the BACKGROUND. Any color can be used, so long as the subject is essentially devoid of that color. The BLUESCREEN PROCESS is a color difference matting process. See BLUESCREEN PROCESS.

COLOR MAP
See LOOKUP TABLE.

COLOR PASS
See BEAUTY PASS.

COLOR REPRODUCTION
The ability of a film stock or compositing process to record or reproduce the colors visible to the human eye.

COLOR SEPARATION PROCESS
The photographic process in which a color image is broken into and then reconstructed from its basic components of red, green and blue light. See COLOR SEPARATIONS.

COLOR SEPARATIONS
Each of three separate pieces of black and white film which record the red, green or blue content of a scene. Color separations are made by passing one of three ADDITIVE PRIMARY COLORS of light (red, green or blue) through a color negative while exposing a piece of black and white film. When red light is used, only the objects in the scene which have some component of red in them are exposed onto the black and white film; when green light is used, only the objects which have some component of green; when blue light is used, only the objects which have some component of blue. The resultant black and white images are referred to as the RED, GREEN or BLUE RECORDS of that scene. Color separations are commonly used as part of the BLUESCREEN PROCESS and also as a method of preserving archival quality films on chemically stable black and white negatives.

COLOR SCALE
See CHIP CHART.

COLOR TABLE
See LOOKUP TABLE.

COLOR TEMPERATURE
A numerical value assigned to a color of light which absolutely identifies that color from all others. The number is equivalent to the temperature to which a pure black object would have to be heated in order to radiate such a color of light. The color temperature of a light source is important in color photography since most color film EMULSIONs are designed to reproduce accurate colors when exposed to either daylight (approximately 6000 degrees kelvin) or tungsten (3200 degrees kelvin) light sources.

COLOR TEST
See COLOR WEDGE.

COLOR TIMING
The process of printing a particular scene or scene ELEMENT such that all colors within the scene appear as they would in the original subject. A scene in which all elements have been color timed properly is COLOR BALANCED.

COLOR TRIANGLE
A triangle which illustrates the relationship between the ADDITIVE (red, green and blue) and SUBTRACTIVE (cyan, magenta and yellow) PRIMARY COLORS of light. The additive primary colors are located on the points of the triangle, while the subtractive primary colors are located on the triangle sides. Each subtractive color is the combination of the two ADDITIVE COLORS on each adjacent point, and is the absence of the additive color on the opposite point. Therefore, if a yellow filter is added to a scene, the blue content of the scene is reduced; if a cyan filter is added, the red content of the scene is reduced; if a magenta filter is added, the green content of the scene is reduced. SImilarly, if red is added to a scene, the scene becomes less cyan; if green is added, the scene becomes less magenta; if blue is added, the scene becomes less yellow.
(See illustration on page 93.)

COLOR WEDGE
A series of test exposures which incrementally alter the color of one or more ELEMENTS in a scene or COMPOSITE. Color wedging is essential in order to achieve a scene in which the colors of all ELEMENTS appear natural in relation to each other.

COMMAND
An instruction issued to a computer.

COMP
Abbreviation for COMPOSITE.

COMPLEMENTARY COLORS
Two colors on opposite sides of the HUE CIRCLE. ADDITIVE COMPLEMENTARY COLORS are mixed together resulting in white; SUBTRACTIVE COMPLEMENTARY COLORS are added together resulting in black.
(See HUE CIRCLE illustration on page 92.)

COMPLEMENTARY MATTES
Any pair of MATTES which are designed to work with each other during COMPOSITE PHOTOGRAPHY. MALE MATTES and FEMALE MATTES are complements of each other as illustrated.

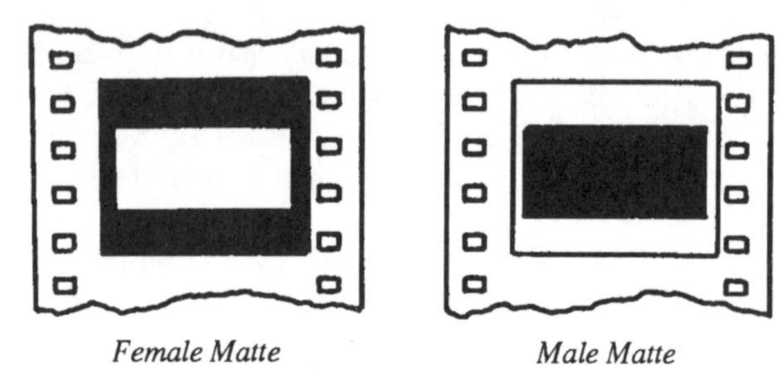

Female Matte *Male Matte*

Complementary Mattes

COMPOSITE
The process or result of taking two or more separate images (ELEMENTS) and combining them onto a third piece of film.

COMPOSITE DUPE
The piece of DUPLICATE NEGATIVE onto which one or more images have been combined.

COMPOSITE PHOTOGRAPHY
The combining of two or more images onto one piece of film using traditional photographic rather than DIGITAL processes.

COMPOSITION
The arrangement of all the ELEMENTS which make up a scene including actors, set pieces, props, light sources and motion. Composition is critical to storytelling and can in itself have an emotional impact on an audience.

COMPSY™
A computerized MULTIPLANE CAMERA system developed by Douglas Trumbull.

COMPUTER ASSISTED ANIMATION
Animation in which the KEY FRAMES are designed by a person while the IN–BETWEENS are created by a computer. The term also applies to computer programs designed to automatically INK AND PAINT drawings which are scanned into the computer.

COMPUTER CHIP
Also called an INTEGRATED CIRCUIT, a device composed of microscopic components which comprise circuits that store and transmit data to and from computers and other electronic devices.

COMPUTER CONTROLLED ANIMATION
See MOTION CONTROL.

COMPUTER FILE
See FILE.

COMPUTER GENERATED ANIMATION
Images which are animated using a computer rather than individually hand drawn.

COMPUTER GENERATED IMAGERY
Any image created with the help of a computer. See COMPUTER GRAPHICS.

COMPUTER GRAPHICS
Any image which is generated using a computer. VECTOR GRAPHICS is an early form of COMPUTER GRAPHICS whereby programmed coordinates are connected in a dot–to–dot fashion to create line drawings. RASTER GRAPHICS uses an array of tiny dots called PIXELS (PICTURE ELEMENTS) which are each assigned a color and brightness. When viewed as a whole, this array of pixels can form very complex images. COMPUTER IMAGE PROCESSING refers to the manipulation of an image using the power of a computer. First the image is DIGITIZED, that is converted to a series of numbers corresponding to the color and brightness of each of many thousands of pixels. Several different types of input devices are available for digitizing an image, including an INPUT SCANNER for flat images such as artwork or film images, and THREE DIMENSIONAL DIGITIZERS for inputting data from a three dimensional model. The numbers are then subjected to "processing;" that is, acted upon by any of thousands of mathematical formulas designed to alter the image in some pre–determined fashion. The digital image is then converted back to a film image by means of an OUTPUT DEVICE. These output devices include HIGH RESOLUTION MONITORS which are photographed with an ordinary film camera and LASER PRINTERS which con-

vert the digital information to a microscopic beam of light which exposes the film negative.

COMPUTER INTERPOLATION
A time saving technique used in COMPUTER GRAPHICS in which the computer creates the "in–between" drawings to complete an action indicated by KEY FRAME ANIMATION.

COMPUTER SCREEN
A MONITOR which serves as the main interface between computer and user. Most computer screens are CATHODE RAY TUBES designed for this specific application.

CONDENSER LENS
A lens commonly used in projectors which gathers light from a wide source (such as a reflective mirror) and concentrates it into a brighter, more controlled beam.

CONTACT PRINTER
A printer in which the EMULSION of the film image to be duplicated is in direct contact with the emulsion of the duplicating stock, i.e., BIPACKED—The bipacked film is then exposed to light, thus transferring the image from one piece of film to the other.

CONTAMINATION
1) In the BLUESCREEN PROCESS, contamination refers to any unwanted exposure in the red and green layers of the film EMULSION in the image area of the bluescreen. Excessive contamination of the red and green layers inhibits the ability to extract good mattes for compositing.
2) Any unwanted exposure to light which could cause a FLASH over a scene, thereby forcing the black VALUES toward gray.

CONTINUITY
The filmmaking concern dealing with consistency of the sound and imagery from shot to shot so as the maintain the illusion that a story is actually filmed as it happens. Continuity involves the action and dialogue of the actors, placement of props and set pieces, overall design, lighting style, etc. In visual effects production continuity primarily concerns the photographic style of the effects in comparison to the live action, or the accuracy of miniatures compared to real props or sets.

CONTRAST
The relative difference between the brightest and darkest areas of an image, including all the intermediate gray tones in between. An image is considered high contrast if there are relatively few tones of gray between opposite extremes of black and white, while an image is low contrast if there are relatively many tones of gray between black and white. Additionally, an image is low contrast or "flat" if the extremes of black and white are absent. Control of contrast in an image is crucial to the successful compositing of an effects shot, and may be manipulated by choice of film stock and processing.

CONTRAST RANGE
A property of a film EMULSION described by the capacity to reproduce a tonal scale from light to dark. An emulsion which can reproduce the extremes of light and dark with few intermediate steps is considered high CONTRAST, while a film stock which can reproduce a wide range of intermediate gray tones is considered low contrast.

CONTROL STRIP
A piece of test film exposed by a SENSITOMETER to yield a range of known exposures from light to dark. This strip is then used to evaluate both the CONTRAST properties of the film stock and the quality of the processing.

COOL
A term used to describe an image which is too blue, or on the 'cool' side of the color spectrum.

COUNTER MATTE
See COMPLEMENTARY MATTE.

CPU
Abbreviation for CENTRAL PROCESSING UNIT.

CRACKER BARREL
A device which vaporizes mineral oil to yield a harmless smoke for effects purposes.

CRASH
The term used to describe the failure of a computer to perform its function due to a mechanical problem or a SOFTWARE BUG. Often times a crash is accompanied by a

painful loss of data which has not been stored in EXTERNAL MEMORY.

CRAWL
The technique of moving text through the frame such as during an end title sequence of a film.

CREATURE SHOP
A facility which creates monsters, robotics, prosthetic makeup effects or animatronic characters.

CROSS DISSOLVE
A transition between scenes in which one image is faded out as a second image is simultaneously faded in. The result is an "overlap" or "crossing" of one image over the other as both receive partial exposure midway through the dissolve. Also referred to as a DISSOLVE or LAP DISSOLVE.

CROSSHAIR DIGITIZER
A hand–held device used in conjunction with a DIGITIZING TABLE or TABLET to input key data points while DIGITIZ-ING a two dimensional drawing. A "crosshair" target is positioned over key points in the drawing while pressing a button to enter the position of that key point on the table. In this manner the computer can then create in memory a dot–to–dot representation of the original drawing.

CROSSOVER
An occurrence during COMPOSITE PHOTOGRAPHY when one image overlaps another thereby requiring a MATTING technique to prevent DOUBLE EXPOSURE or PRINT THROUGH.

CROSSOVER SHEET
A log which records the various frames at which one ELE-MENT of a COMPOSITE crosses over a second, therefore requiring a MATTE to prevent PRINT THROUGH.

CRT
Abbreviation for CATHODE RAY TUBE.

CRYSTAL MOTOR
A self–regulating motor whose speed is controlled by the use of crystal oscillators.

CURSOR
A symbol used to designate the point on a computer screen where the next action will take place. Such actions include the typing of characters or lines or the application of paint in a PAINT PROGRAM.

CUTOUT ANIMATION
An animation technique which utilizes cut out shapes or figures which are then incrementally manipulated for the camera to photograph one frame at a time.

CYAN
One of the SUBTRACTIVE PRIMARY COLORS used in OPTICAL PRINTING. Cyan light is produced by subtracting primary red from white light. The addition of cyan to a scene is equivalent to removing red. See COLOR TRIANGLE.

CYC
Abbreviation and common name for a CYCLORAMA.

CYCLE
See ANIMATION CYCLE.

CYCLE ANIMATION
See ANIMATION CYCLE.

CYCLORAMA
A large fabric backdrop (more commonly referred to as a CYC) which is stretched across the BACKGROUND of a scene. Cycloramas range from relatively simple neutral colors simulating a sky to elaborate paintings of landscapes or cityscapes. The more elaborate cycloramas are generally referred to as BACKINGS.

DAILIES
1) The processed film, prepared for screening, which results from the previous day of shooting.
2) The regularly scheduled daily screening of film which was shot the previous day. Also called RUSHES.

DAILY REPORT
A report issued daily which summarizes the work to be done on a series of shots as discussed in the screening of DAILIES.

DATA
Binary information which is stored, transmitted or otherwise manipulated by a computer or electronic device.

DATABASE
An organized collection of data or records stored on a computer memory device.

DAY FOR NIGHT
A photographic procedure which uses UNDEREXPOSURE and special filters to simulate night lighting conditions in full daylight.

DAYLIGHT BALANCED FILM
Color film stock which is chemically balanced to reproduce accurate colors when exposed under daylight conditions. See COLOR TEMPERATURE.

DEBUGGING
The process of identifying and correcting flaws (BUGS) in computer HARDWARE and SOFTWARE.

DEFINITION
The sharpness or level of detail apparent in an image as affected by the quality of optics, AERIAL PERSPECTIVE or special filtration.

DEFORMATION
The COMPUTER ANIMATION technique of changing the shape of an object to create the illusion of movement between frames.

DEGAUSSER
A device which erases large quantities of magnetic tape.

DEGRADATION
The loss of quality in color, CONTRAST and definition whenever an image is duplicated or manipulated in any way.

DENSITOMETER
An optical instrument which measures the opacity of a film image. DENSITOMETRY plays an important part in determining proper BLUESCREEN exposure and MATTE density.

DENSITOMETRY
The process of measuring the density of a film image using a DENSITOMETER.

DENSITY
The opacity of a film image. An image which transmits no light has maximum density, while a transparent image has no density whatsoever.

DEPTH CUEING
The COMPUTER GRAPHICS process of assigning an intensity to an object according to its distance from an imaginary viewer. The effect is that of creating AERIAL PERSPECTIVE in the image. See AERIAL PERSPECTIVE.

DEPTH OF FIELD
The range of acceptable focus which extends both in front of and behind the principal subject of a scene. Depth of field is controllable to some extent through the selection of lens focal length and lens APERTURE.

DESATURATION
A term used to describe the loss of color during duplication or FLASHING of an image. The degree of color saturation is an important consideration during the COMPOSITING of a multiple ELEMENT shot. At times a scene is intentionally desaturated to yield a specific photographic style.

DETAIL
See DEFINITION.

DIFFERENCE MATTE
A MATTE created during the application of DIFFERENCE MATTING techniques.

DIFFERENCE MATTING
A process which isolates individual ELEMENTS of a single image by comparing the differences between the image elements. The BLUESCREEN PROCESS (COLOR DIFFERENCE MATTING) uses the difference between the blue BACKGROUND and the non–blue foreground to optically separate the images. With the advent of DIGITAL technology a more subtle variation of difference matting is possible. Two images which are similar but for slight differences, such as a single foreground character, can be compared PIXEL by PIXEL. In this way the differences between the two images,

i.e., the single character, can be isolated for treatment by the computer.

DIFFUSION FILTER
A special piece of glass, plastic or other material placed over the lens of a taking camera to soften the edges of an image and eliminate detail. Known as a LOW PASS FILTER in COMPUTER GRAPHICS.

DIGITAL
1) An electronic state consisting of ones and zeros.
2) Information in the form of the numerical digits one and zero which is meaningful to a computer.
3) Any equipment or processes controlled or executed by a computer using digital information is described as a "digital" process or "digital" equipment.

DIGITAL ANIMATION
Animation which is created using COMPUTER GRAPHICS techniques. See COMPUTER GRAPHICS.

DIGITAL COMPOSITE
A COMPOSITE of images which is executed by a computer as opposed to more traditional photographic processes.

DIGITAL IMAGE
An imaginary image in the form of binary information stored in a computer which is only visible when output to another format such as film or videotape.

DIGITAL PRINTER
See OUTPUT DEVICE.

DIGITAL VIDEO
Video images which are recorded as a series of discrete points of image information known as PICTURE ELEMENTS or PIXELS. D1 and D2 are both DIGITAL video formats.

DIGITAL VIDEO COMPOSITE
A videotape COMPOSITE using DIGITAL video equipment.

DIGITAL VIDEO EFFECTS
Video effects including zooms, reductions, flips, tumbles, page turns, etc., which are created on any number of pieces of DIGITAL video equipment.

DIGITIZE
The process of converting real two-dimensional images or three-dimensional objects into an array of BINARY numbers which a computer can then manipulate. Two dimensional images are digitized using an INPUT SCANNER which reads a finite number of points of information, called PIXELS, and assigns numbers corresponding to the brightness and color of each point. A DIGITIZING TABLE or TABLET, in combination with a CROSSHAIR DIGITIZER, can be used to input line drawings or two dimensional graphics into a computer. THREE DIMENSIONAL DIGITIZING utilizes either a DIGITIZING PEN which is traced over the major profiles of all three dimensions of a model, or a VIDEO DIGITIZER which records the relief of an object. Three dimensional digitizing is limited to form only, color and brightness having to be assigned to each pixel as a separate procedure.

DIGITIZING PEN
An electronic pen whose position on or above a DIGITIZING TABLE/TABLET is tracked by a computer using magnetic field disturbances. Also called a STYLUS, the pen is used to trace the outline of two dimensional graphics or three dimensional objects in order to locate key points along the graphic or object. The computer then interpolates the positions between the various key points to yield a DIGITAL approximation of the original.
(See illustration on page 38.)

DIGITIZING SCANNER
See INPUT SCANNER.

DIGITIZING TABLE/TABLET
An electronic drawing pad used to transfer two–dimensional graphic shapes into a computer. Generally using a DIGITIZING PEN, a MOUSE, or a CROSSHAIR DIGITIZER, the shape of an object is entered as a series of KEY POINTS relative to a coordinate system which the computer uses to divide the table top into a series of addressable points. The computer then connects the key points with straight lines in order to approximate the original subject.

D–1 FORMAT
The highest quality format for storing a video image. The equivalent of a film NEGATIVE, a D–1 image has not suf-

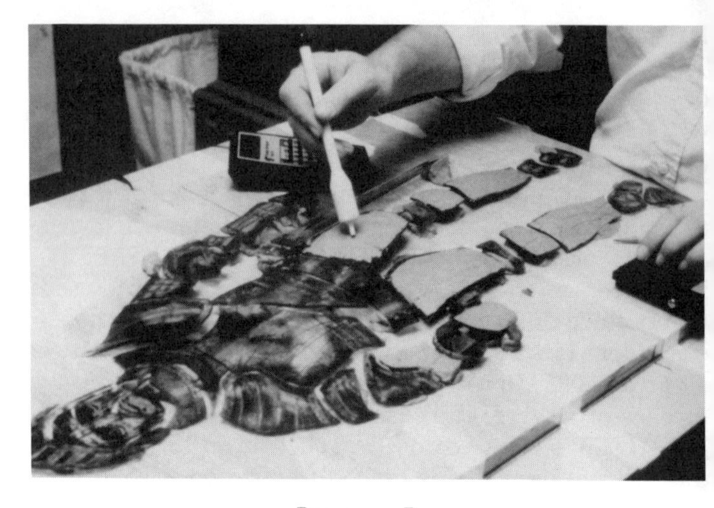

DIGITIZING PEN
A digitizing pen is used to trace the basic shape of an object into a computer, in this case, the stained glass man from "Young Sherlock Holmes." The result of this tracing can be seen in the illustration for WIREFRAME on page 150. Photo courtesy of Paramount Pictures.

fered the loss of quality inherent in the process of encoding the image for broadcast. For this reason, this format is the preferred storage medium during editing and compositing operations. The D–1 image may be copied endlessly without degradation, however before broadcast the image must be encoded and converted to D–2, resulting in a significant loss of quality. See also D–2 FORMAT.

DIOPTER LENS
An auxiliary lens which is placed over the front of an ordinary lens to achieve extreme close focusing.

DIRTY DUPE
A quick but low quality copy of a scene or sequence which is used for reference purposes only.

DISKETTE
The common 5-1/4" and 3-1/2" FLOPPY DISCS used as memory storage devices with personal computers.

DISPLACEMENT MAPPING
The COMPUTER GRAPHICS process of displacing the surface of an object to create an actual surface texture, as opposed to texture simulation accomplished with BUMP MAPPING.

DISPLAY
A video MONITOR is used to show or "display" an image stored in computer memory or on video tape. See also COMPUTER SCREEN.

DISSOLVE
See CROSS DISSOLVE.

DOUBLE DUPE
An image which is a copy made from a copy of the original negative. The double duped image suffers significant loss of quality.

DOUBLE EXPOSURE
The exposure of two images onto the same piece of film without the benefit of MATTING techniques. Double exposure allows each image to be seen or "PRINT THROUGH" the other.

DOUBLE FRAME
The occurrence of the same image on two sucessive frames of film either intentionally or due to a SINGLE FRAME CAMERA malfunction.

DOUBLE FRAMING
The technique of printing each frame twice in order to slow down the action in a scene.

DOUBLE PASS PHOTOGRAPHY
See FRONT LIT BACK LIT.

DOUBLE PRINTING
See DOUBLE FRAMING.

DOUBLE SYSTEM
A method of screening the picture and sound rolls of an unfinished film by using separate film projection and sound playback machines which are electronically synchronized.

DOWNLOAD
The process of transferring data from bulk storage into the active memory of a computer device. The opposite is called UPLOADING.

DROP OUT
The momentary loss of a portion of a video picture. Dropouts are visible as small white or black flashes or streaks running horizontally through the frame.

DRY ICE MACHINE
A container of hot water into which dry ice (frozen carbon dioxide) is introduced to create a low lying fog.

D–2 FORMAT
A video image storage format which is the result of the encoding of D–1 for broadcast. Since the encoding process reduces the quality of the image, D–2 is of lesser quality than D–1. See also D–1 FORMAT.

DUB
See DUBBING.

DUBBING
The process of making a copy of a video image.

DUMP TANKS
Specially built water tanks which can empty their contents quickly to create a flood.

DUPE
1) Abbreviation for DUPLICATE or DUPLICATE NEGATIVE.
2) A copy of any original is called a "dupe" (short for "duplicate.")
3) The process of making a copy from an original.

DUPE NEG
Abbreviation for DUPLICATE NEGATIVE.

DUPLICATE NEGATIVE
A copy of the ORIGINAL NEGATIVE made onto high quality film stock. A COMPOSITE of a multiple ELEMENT shot is a duplicate negative.

DVE
Abbreviation for DIGITAL VIDEO EFFECTS.

DX
Abbreviation for DOUBLE EXPOSURE.

DYKSTRAFLEX™
A MOTION CONTROL TRACK CAMERA developed under the leadership of John Dykstra for the filming of miniatures for STAR WARS. See TRACK CAMERA.

DYNAMIC RANGE
The range of colors and values a computer is capable of representing based upon the number of BITS which are used to record each color. The greater the number of bits per PIXEL, the greater the dynamic range. High end COMPUTER GRAPHICS SOFTWARE systems assign 24 bits per pixel to create well over sixteen million different color and value combinations.

EAGLE DRIVE™
A computer disc drive which holds 330 megabytes of data.

EASE IN/OUT
The process of making smooth camera or subject moves by slowly accelerating to full speed and then decelerating to a stop. The term is often used by animators as well as by live action crews.

EAST
A term borrowed from the compass referring to the right hand portion of an image or frame. See FIELD CHART.

EDGE CHARACTERISTICS
The term which loosely defines the appearance of the edges of an image which has been matted into a scene. The term specifically refers to the character of the edges of an image that a particular film stock is capable of reproducing. For example, high CONTRAST black and white stocks generally produce an edge which is sharper or "harder" than a low contrast stock.

EDGE CODE
Sequential numbers which are custom printed onto the edges of a piece of film after the film has been developed. Identical edge code numbers are typically printed onto matching sound and picture film in order to maintain the sync relationship after the film has been edited into smaller pieces. See also EDGE NUMBERS.

EDGE DETECTION
An automated technique in COMPUTER GRAPHICS in which the edges of a subject in an image are identified in order to separate the subject from the BACKGROUND.

EDGE NUMBERS
Sequential numbers exposed into the EMULSION of negative film stock during manufacture and later transferred to workprints during printing. Edge numbers appear along the edge of a strip of film at one foot intervals and allow filmmakers to clearly identify any particular frame from all others. Also called KEY NUMBERS, they differ from EDGE CODE in that edge numbers are for picture only and are an integral part of the manufacture of the film, while EDGE CODE is used on both picture and sound and is applied at the discretion of the editorial staff. Edge numbers are for the identification of corresponding frames of positive and negative, while EDGE CODE is used to maintain a sync relationship of picture and sound after a long piece of film is cut during editing.

EFFECTS
A short hand reference to SPECIAL VISUAL EFFECTS.

EFFECTS ANIMATION
SPECIAL VISUAL EFFECTS which are created through various animation techniques such as CEL ANIMATION or SLIT SCAN photography.

EFFECTS CAMERA
An ANIMATION STAND which is used to create visual effects using techniques other than cel animation. SLIT SCAN and STREAK PHOTOGRAPHY are examples of effects camera techniques.

EFFECTS FILM
Generic term for the genre of films which employ a great deal of VISUAL EFFECTS.

EFFECTS FILTER
Photographic tools as simple as a clear plastic bag or as complicated as a specially faceted piece of glass which are placed in front of the lens of a taking camera to achieve a special effect such as diffusion, multi–image, or starbursts effects, etc.

EFFECTS SHOT
Any shot which contains an effect which is principally created in post–production.

EIGHT BIT COLOR
Refers to the number of color possibilities for COMPUTER GENERATED IMAGERY when each PIXEL is stored as eight BITS of information, or 256 different colors. See COLOR DEPTH, SIXTEEN BIT COLOR, TWENTY–FOUR BIT COLOR and THIRTY–TWO BIT COLOR.

EIGHT PERF
A nickname for the VISTAVISION FORMAT. The term comes from the fact that each frame of film has eight pairs of perforations.

EIKONIX™
An INPUT SCANNING device used to DIGITIZE film images.

ELECTRONIC CLAPPER
See BLOOP LIGHT.

ELECTRONIC COMPOSITING
The combining of images using video compositing equipment.

ELEMENT
A single image which is to be combined with others during COMPOSITE PHOTOGRAPHY. For example, a star field, a planet and a space vehicle are all elements which make up a space adventure EFFECTS SHOT.

EMPIRE HIGH SPEED CAMERA™
A HIGH SPEED version of the EMPIRE SOUND SPEED CAMERA.

EMPIRE SOUND SPEED CAMERA™
A SOUND SPEED VISTAVISION camera built by Industrial Light and Magic company and named after "The Empire Strikes Back."

EMULSION
The photosensitive layers of silver halides which are the foundation of modern photography. Motion picture color film emulsions are comprised of three distinct layers each sensitive to one of the three primary colors of light: red, green and blue. These emulsion layers are applied to a film base of either cellulose acetate or polyester which is coated with an anti–halation backing. The BLUESCREEN PROCESS relies heavily on the fact that each of the three layers of the film

emulsion are individually exposed by a different PRIMARY COLOR of light.

ENCODER
An optical/electronic device which is commonly used in MOTION CONTROL equipment to measure the rotation of the shaft of a motor.

ENCORE™
A DIGITAL VIDEO EFFECTS device manufactured by Quantel.

ESTAR BASE
A sturdy and tear resistant film base upon which an EMULSION is then placed. Estar based film stocks are used in visual effects applications where precise REGISTRATION is mandatory or when repeated passes through a camera would put excessive wear on the perforations of an ACETATE BASED film.

EV READING
A measure of the light reflected off a subject. EV literally means EXPOSURE VALUE.

EXABYTE
A tape storage medium which holds 2.2 gigabytes of information.

EXACT CUT
The precise length of an effects shot as it is going to be used in a film. "Exact cut" information is critical in order to avoid wasting time and money on frames of a shot which will not be used in the movie.

EXPOSE
The act of allowing light to strike an undeveloped negative for the purpose of creating a photographic image.

EXPOSED FILM
A film EMULSION which has already been "exposed" to light and is ready for processing.

EXPOSURE
The measure of the amount of light to which a film EMULSION is exposed. A scene which needs to appear bright is given "more exposure" while a scene which needs to appear dark is given "less exposure."

EXPOSURE BRACKETING
See EXPOSURE WEDGE.

EXPOSURE SHEET
An instructional log used in conjunction with cel animation indicating which cels should be photographed on each frame of film. Exposure sheets also dictate any camera movement.

EXPOSURE VALUE
A number which relates to the amount of light reflecting off a subject. Exposure value takes into account both the reflective quality of the subject and the amount of light striking the subject. Exposure values are obtained using a REFLECTIVE LIGHT METER.

EXPOSURE WEDGE
The practice of exposing successive frames of film to different intensities or duration of light to determine which exposure level is appropriate. This practice is also called EXPOSURE BRACKETING.

EXTERNAL MEMORY
A data storage device such as an OPTICAL DISC or MAGNETIC TAPE which augments the internal storage capacity of a computer.

FADE IN/OUT
An optical effect used as a scene transition. A scene "fades out" if it becomes progressively darker until it reaches black. A scene "fades in" if it starts out black and increasingly becomes lighter until full exposure is achieved.

FEMALE MATTE
A MATTE used in OPTICAL PRINTING which features a clear silhouette of a foreground subject against a field of black. Other names for this type of matte are CLEAR CENTER MATTE, CLEAR CORE MATTE, COVER MATTE, BURN–IN MATTE and HOLD BACK MATTE. See BLUESCREEN PROCESS.
(See illustration on page 46 and color photograph on page 91.)

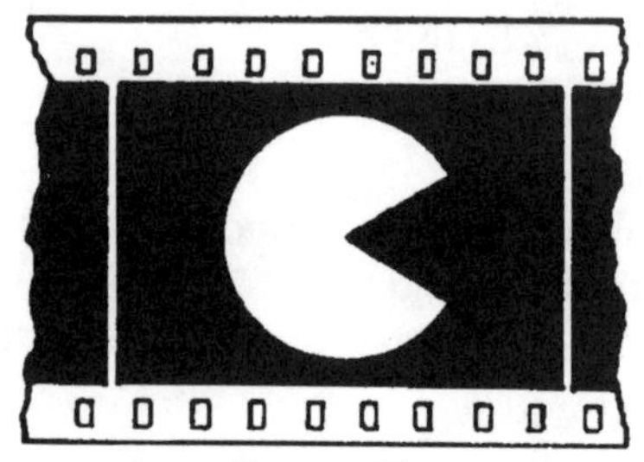

FEMALE MATTE

FG
Abbreviation of FOREGROUND.

FIBER OPTICS
A system of flexible glass tubes which transmit through their entire lengths nearly all the light which enters one end. Fiber optics are used in modelmaking to conveniently create a complex series of small PRACTICAL lights from a single light source.

FIELD
1) The area of view of a taking lens, ie: FIELD OF VIEW.
2) A unit of measure on a FIELD CHART.
3) One half of a video image. Each field of a 525 line resolution video image is composed of every other SCAN LINE, containing 262-1/2 lines total. These fields are INTERLACED to form the complete image.

FIELD CHART
A grid which serves to divide the frame into quadrants addressable by north/south and east/west coordinates. Each camera and viewing system to be used in the composition of an effects shot can be fitted with this grid to aid in the accurate positioning of shot ELEMENTS.

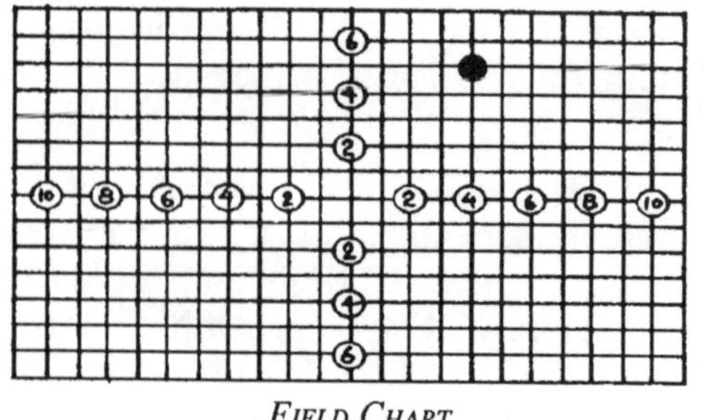

Point indicated is East 4, North 5.

FIELD CHART

FIELD OF VIEW
The area to be photographed by a TAKING CAMERA.

FIELD RECORDER
A system which employs a computer and a specially modified gear head which allows the computer to record the camera moves performed by a live action operator. The computer can then repeat the move at a later date for MATCHED–MOVE PHOTOGRAPHY of additional ELEMENTS.

FIELD SIZE
The size of an image as measured by the grid of a FIELD CHART.

FIFTY–FIFTY MIRROR
A semi–reflective (and semi–transparent) mirror commonly used in special effects photography. Fifty-fifty refers to the fact that 50 percent of the light striking this mirror is reflected while 50 percent is transmitted. This type of mirror is also referred to as a BEAM SPLITTER or a HALF-SILVERED MIRROR. The degree of transmission verses reflectance can be controlled during manufacture to yield for instance a 40/60 or a 20/80 mirror. Mirrors of this type are commonly positioned at a 45 degree angle in front of a camera lens in order to simultaneously film two separate images. The image directly in front of the camera is partially transmitted through the mirror to the camera lens, while an image to the side of the camera is partially reflected into the camera lens.

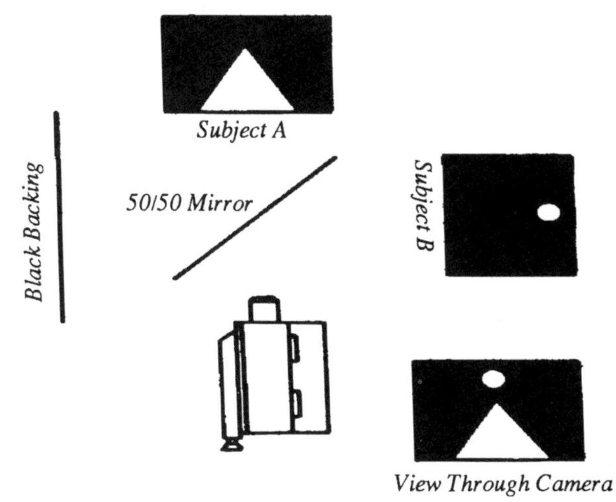

Fifty-Fifty Mirror Setup

5272 COMPOSITE
A nickname given to a quick and rough color COMPOSITE used to verify that the various ELEMENTS of a shot are working in conjunction with each other. The name is derived from the Kodak film stock number which is used for these composites. Also called 5272, 5272 COMP, or ROUGH COMPOSITE.

FILE
A collection of data or instructions for use by a computer.

FILM CHAIN
A device used to transfer film images to videotape. Also called a TELECINE.

FILM GATE
The portion of a camera or projector movement in which the film is positioned for exposure. See CAMERA MOVEMENT.

FILM LOOP
A length of film which has been joined at the ends such that it forms an endless loop when projected. Film loops are useful for repeatedly viewing a shot for study without having to back the projector up or rethread.

FILM MAGAZINE
The light proof chamber fastened to a camera which houses film both before and after it has been exposed.

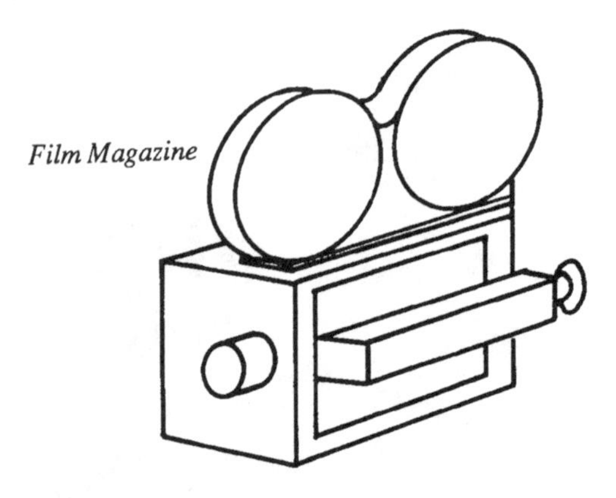

FILM MAGAZINE

FILM MOVEMENT
See CAMERA MOVEMENT.

FILM PITCH
See PERFORATION PITCH.

FILM SCANNER
An INPUT SCANNING device for converting film images into an array of numbers which a computer can then manipulate. See COMPUTER GRAPHICS and DIGITIZE.

FINAL
A name given to a COMPOSITE which is deemed suitable both technically and creatively for use in a motion picture.

FINAL CUT
The final version (hopefully) of an edited motion picture.

FIRST GENERATION COPY
The first print or copy made from an ORIGINAL NEGATIVE or MASTER.

FISH EYE LENS
A lens which takes in a field of view of nearly 180 degrees. An image filmed with such a lens appears distorted when projected onto a flat surface. Objects close to camera take prominence and suffer severe elongation of features.

FIXED HARD DISC
A DISC DRIVE which is permanently installed in a computer.

FIXED MATTE
A MATTE which does not change shape or position during the course of a shot, as opposed to a TRAVELING MATTE.

FIXED SHUTTER
A non–variable camera shutter.

FLARE
Any of a wide range of light flashes or fogging effects which cover all or a portion of the frame. Light flares typically indicate that the camera is nearly pointed into a light source, such as the sun.

FLASH
A low level of light to which an unprocessed negative is exposed for the purpose of reducing the CONTRAST or the COLOR SATURATION of a scene.

FLASH FRAME
A single frame within a scene which has been grossly overexposed relative to other frames either accidentally or intentionally in order to identify a segment of film which follows.

FLASHING
The process of exposing a piece of unprocessed negative to a low level of light in order to reduce CONTRAST or COLOR SATURATION of a scene. Also called FOGGING.

FLAT FOUR
Abbreviation for FLAT LENS FOUR PERF which refers to the standard motion picture format of SPHERICAL (FLAT LENS) FOUR PERF (35 mm) film.

FLAT LENS
See SPHERICAL LENS.

FLICKER
A rhythmic pulsing of exposure in a motion picture image caused by a camera malfunction, improper sync with HMI lighting, improperly trimmed arc lamps or defective film stock. Flicker becomes a terminal problem whenever you wish to MATTE a non–flickering image over a BACKGROUND which has flicker.

FLIP
See OPTICAL FLIP.

FLOPPY DISC
Portable discs of magnetic film used to store small amounts of computer data. The 5-1/4″ and 3-1/2″ diskettes common to home computers are examples.

FLYING
See WIREWORK.

FLYING SPOT SCANNER
A film–to–videotape transfer device which uses an electronic beam to scan the film images while the film is continuously moving past the electron beam.

FOAMCORE
A fairly durable cardboard with a styrofoam core which is commonly used in model making.

FOG FILTER
A special effects filter which produces a subtle glow around light sources within the frame and a general softening of the overall image.

FOGGING
See FLASHING.

FOOT
The end of a roll of film.

FORCED DEVELOPMENT
An extension of the normal processing time allotted for a film EMULSION in order to compensate for underexposure of the negative. Also called OVERDEVELOPMENT or PUSHING.

FORCED PERSPECTIVE
A technique employed in set design whereby the depth of the set is artificially enhanced by placing incrementally smaller scale details at incrementally greater distances from the camera. The small details in the distance then appear to be at a greater distance from the camera than they actually are.

FOREGROUND
Loosely refers to an ELEMENT of a shot which appears closer to the camera than all others.In COMPOSITE PHOTOGRAPHY it specifically refers to the ELEMENT to be matted over all others.

FOREGROUND MATTE
See FEMALE MATTE.

FORESHORTENING
The artificial compression of depth achieved by filming through a telephoto lens. The effect is that distant subjects appear closer to camera with less space between successively more distant objects.

FORMAT
1) The ASPECT RATIO of a projected image.
2) The size of a piece of film as measured in millimeters across the width. For example: 16 mm, 35 mm, 70 mm. Also known as the GAUGE of the film.
(See illustrations on pages 52-53.)

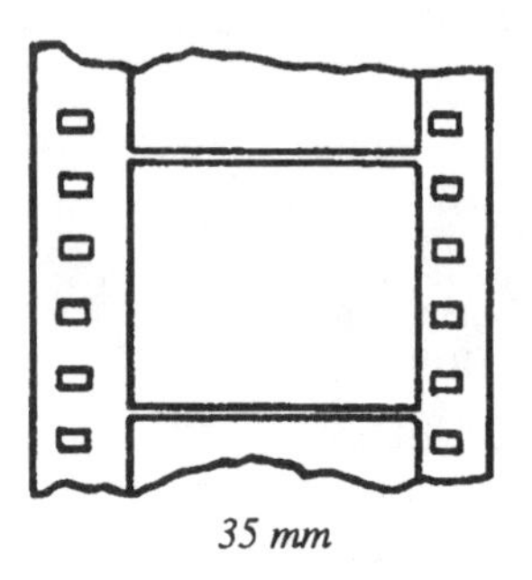

35 mm

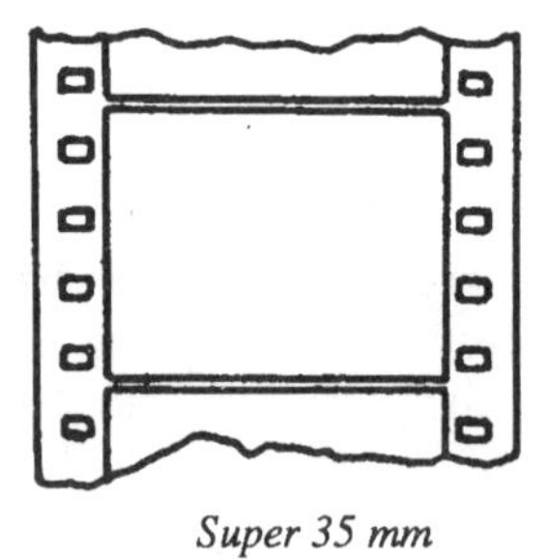

Super 35 mm

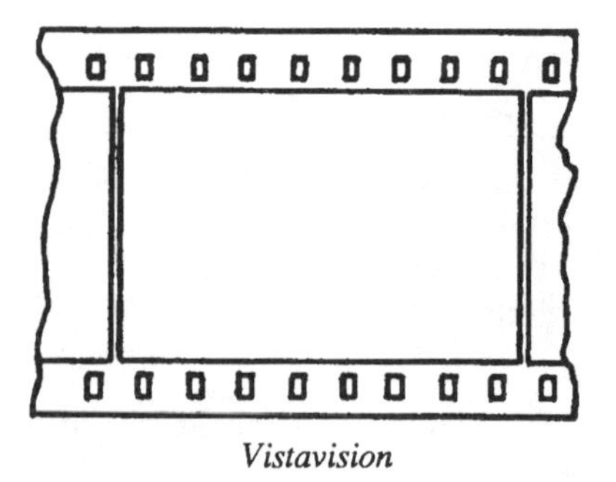

Vistavision

Film Formats

Actual Size

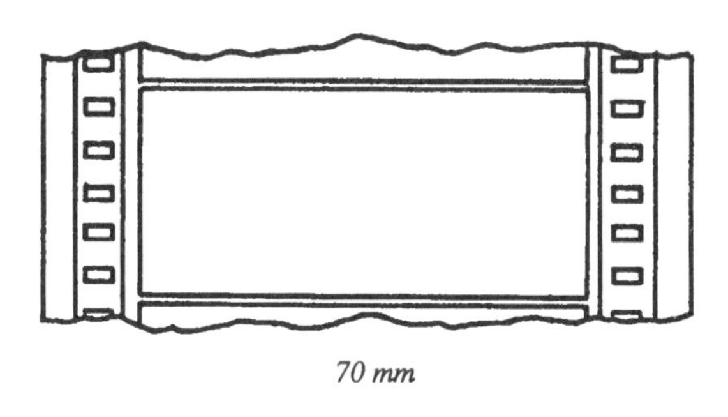

70 mm

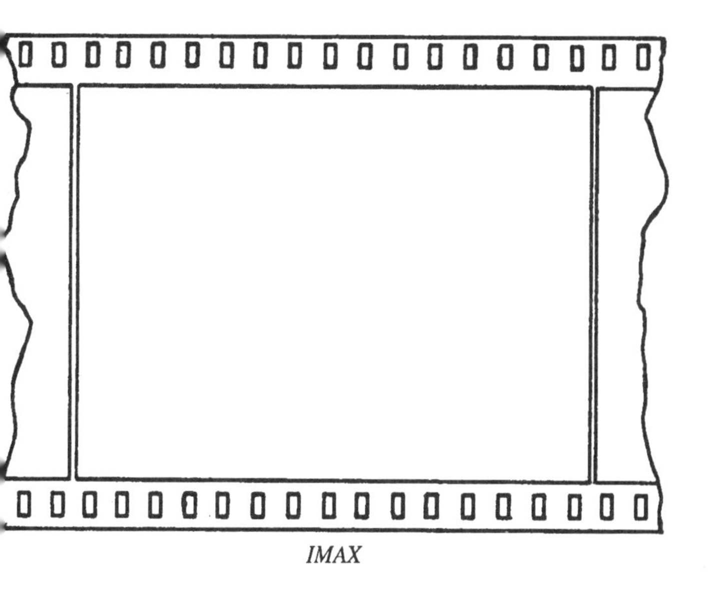

IMAX

Film Formats

Actual Size

FOUR BY FIVE CAMERA
A still camera which exposes a four inch by five inch negative yielding very high RESOLUTION and DETAIL.

FOUR PERF
Nickname for standard 35 mm FILM GAUGE born of the fact that each FRAME of film has four pairs of PERFORATIONS.

FP
Abbreviation for FRONT PROJECTION.

FPS
Abbreviation for FRAMES PER SECOND.

FRACTAL
A component of a computer generated image that, when repeated, forms a greater image of essentially the same character. For example a single branch of a tree, when repeated and positioned properly, could be used over and over again to create the entire tree.

FRAME
One of the individual images which, when combined with others, make up a motion picture.
(See illustration on page 55.)

FRAME BUFFER
Special computer memory which stores a single frame image while it is not immediately required for processing during COMPUTER GRAPHICS operations.

FRAME CAPTURE
See FRAME GRAB.

FRAME GRAB
To input a single video frame into a computer using a FRAME GRABBER.

FRAME GRABBER
A device used to transfer individual frames of video into a computer.

FRAME LINE
The line which appears on all motion picture film delineating the individual frames.

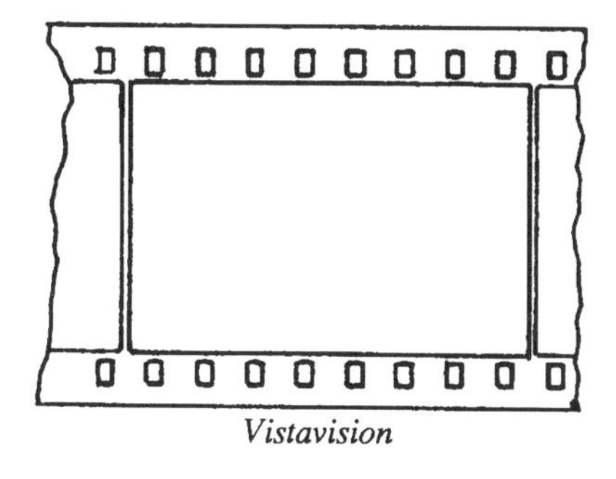

Vistavision

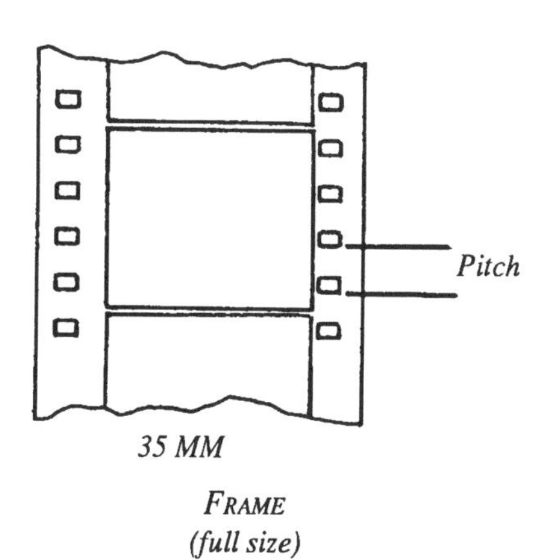

35 MM

FRAME
(full size)

RAME RATE
he rate at which frames of film are exposed. Frame rates are
ıeasured in units of frames per second, with a standard rate
f 24.

RAMES PER SECOND
he unit of measure for the rate at which film is exposed.
.bbreviated as FPS.

RAME STORE
. device used to store individual images for use at a later
me. Also called a STILL STORE or FRAME BUFFER.

REEZE FRAME (PRINTING)
. printing procedure in which a single frame of an action
:ene is repeatedly printed in order to "freeze" the action.

FRINGING

1) A halo which appears around the edges of a foreground subject which has been improperly matted into a scene.
2) A blue halo which appears around the subject of a BLUESCREEN ELEMENT.

FRONT LIGHT/BACK LIGHT

See FRONT LIT/BACK LIT.

FRONT LIT/BACK LIT

A self MATTING technique in which a subject with REPEAT-ABLE motion is first filmed with front lighting (BEAUTY PASS) and subsequently filmed against a white card or back light source while remaining unlit (MATTE PASS). The MATTE pass results in a silhouette of the subject against a clear BACKGROUND, which can then be used for compositing.

FRONT LIT BLUESCREEN

A BLUESCREEN made of blue fabric or a painted surface which is lit from the front. Front lit bluescreens are common in video processes and are sometimes used for film as well

FRONT PROJECTION

A process of filming primarily live action scenes in a confined studio space while projecting images of the BACKGROUND onto a screen behind the actors. The BACKGROUND images are limitless and can be produced with any number of live action or special effects techniques. Front projection differs from REAR PROJECTION in that the BACKGROUND image is projected from the front of the screen with the help of a FIFTY–FIFTY MIRROR. The taking camera sees both the actor and the BACKGROUND to create the illusion that they were originally filmed at the same time. See REAR PROJECTION and INTROVISION.

(See illustration on page 57.)

FRONT PROJECTION BLUESCREEN

A process of BLUESCREEN PHOTOGRAPHY in which blue light is projected onto a FRONT PROJECTION SCREEN to serve as the blue backing. This technique has advantages over the traditional front lit or rear lit bluescreens in cases where the subject is highly reflective and might be contaminated by reflections of the bluescreen.

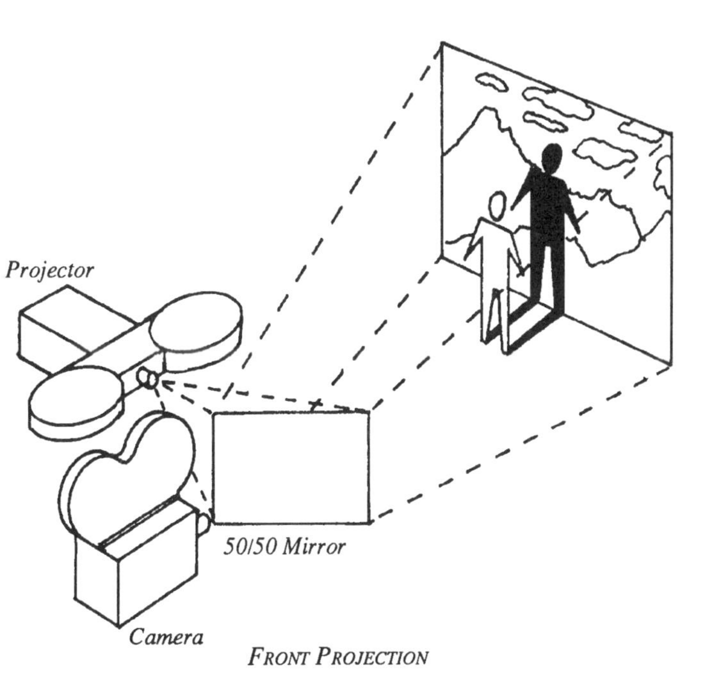

FRONT PROJECTION

FRONT PROJECTION PHOTOGRAPHY
See FRONT PROJECTION.

FRONT PROJECTION PROCESS
See FRONT PROJECTION.

FRONT PROJECTION SCREEN
A highly reflective surface made up of microscopic glass beads which reflect most of the light which strike them back into the direction of the light source. The most common front projection screen carries the trademarked name Scotchlite. See BEADED SCREEN.

FULL APERTURE
The largest image area available for filming in any particular format. "Full aperture" usually refers to the 35 mm format in cases where the photographed image extends into the area normally reserved for the sound track.
(See FORMAT ILLUSTRATION on pages 52-53.)

FX
Abbreviation for EFFECTS, SPECIAL EFFECTS or SPECIAL VISUAL EFFECTS.

GAMMA
The objective measurement of CONTRAST of an image. Gamma is dependent upon the development time and strength of chemicals used and is equal to the slope of the CHARACTERISTIC CURVE.

GAMMA CORRECTION
The process of adjusting the brightness variation of a DIGITAL IMAGE to be DISPLAYED on a video MONITOR to compensate for the inherent inability of the color phosphors used in a CRT to produce a smooth GRAY SCALE.

GAMMA CURVE
See CHARACTERISTIC CURVE.

GARBAGE MATTE
An animated MATTE which isolates a subject from unwanted imagery included in the original photography. A garbage matte is typically used to remove lighting fixtures, grip equipment or any other "garbage" which is not to be part of a COMPOSITED image. See BLUESCREEN PROCESS.
(See photo on page 90.)

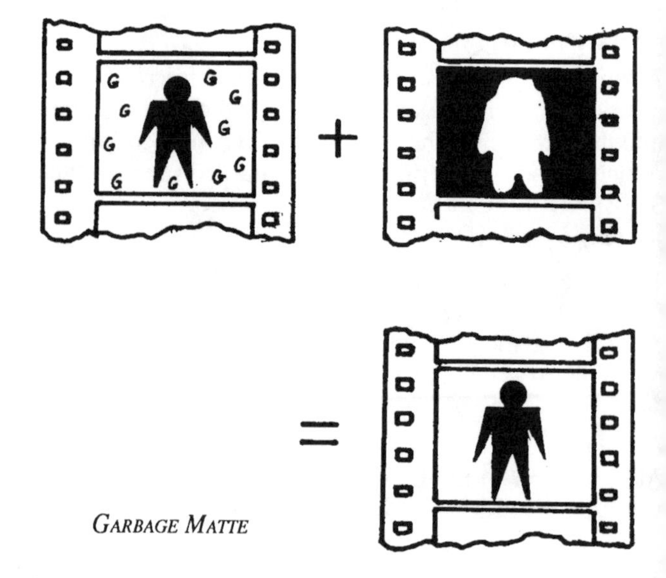

GARBAGE MATTE

GATE
See FILM GATE.

GAUGE
The size of a piece of film as measured in millimeters across the width. For example: 16 mm, 35 mm, 70 mm.
(See FORMAT ILLUSTRATION on pages 52-53.)

GENERATION
Reference given to the number of copies which have been made from an ORIGINAL NEGATIVE. The original negative is referred to as "first generation," the first duplicate is referred to as "second generation," the second duplicate is referred to as "third generation," and so forth.

GENERATION LOSS
The loss of quality in an image due to duplication.

GHOST IMAGE
A dim secondary image which seems to be slightly offset or delayed from the primary image. Ghost images are sometimes accidently caused by internal reflections of a lens, or intentionally created with DOUBLE EXPOSURE.

GHOSTING
See GHOST IMAGE.

GIGABYTE
One thousand MEGABYTES; one billion BYTES.

GIMBLE
A device upon which a set or prop is placed in order to be rocked back and forth, right and left.

GIRL HEAD
An old–fashioned, however commonly used term relating to an image of a woman with typical anglo skin tone. The "girl head" image is placed at the head of a LAB ROLL to evaluate the quality of color reproduction during any particular processing operation. Also called KODAK GIRL.

GLASS SHOT
A technique of special effects photography which involves placing a large piece of glass between the camera and the principal subject to be filmed. The glass is then painted with a scene which extends or elaborates upon the live action. This

technique consumes considerable set time, and for this reason is seldom used for major motion pictures.

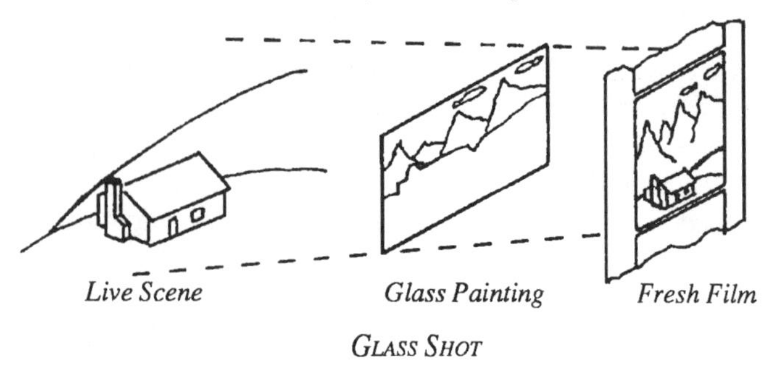

GLASS SHOT

GLITCH
A catch–all name given to any momentary defect in an image. Glitches comes in all sizes and shapes and are caused by an infinite number of mistakes or conditions.

GLOW PASS
An auxiliary pass to the BEAUTY PASS which generally accomplishes some sort of glowing effect on the subject being photographed. A glow pass often uses strong point sources of light in conjunction with diffusion or fog filters. An example of a glow pass would be any of the space ship engine lights from the "Star Wars" trilogy.

G MATTE
Abbreviation for GARBAGE MATTE.

GO–MOTION
An outgrowth of MOTION CONTROL photography and the need to eliminate the strobing common in STOP MOTION ANIMATION. Go–motion employs a motion control computer and various motors, linkages, cables and levers to mechanically manipulate a stop motion puppet during exposure. The movement of the puppet is choreographed by the go–motion animator through the use of a joystick. The computer then repeats the motion, one frame at a time, while each frame of film is being exposed. The result is essentially stop motion animation which includes the motion blur necessary for a more realistic effect.

GRAIN
The silver halide particles which make up a film EMULSION. Although they are microscopic in size, when projected on a

arge screen they are visible as moving particles in the image. The visible GRAININESS of the film is increased with each GENERATION.

GRAININESS
The subjective appearance of a filmed image to appear coarse or "grainy."

GRAIN–OF–RICE BULB
A light bulb the size of a grain of rice often used as working lights in miniatures.

GRAIN–OF–WHEAT BULB
A light bulb the size of a grain of wheat often used as working lights in miniatures.

GRAPHIC INPUT DEVICE
See DIGITIZE, DIGITIZING TABLE/TABLET and INPUT SCANNER.

GRAPHIC OUTPUT DEVICE
Any device used to DISPLAY or make HARD COPIES of computer imagery. Such devices include a MONITOR, SOLITAIRE, and LASER PRINTER.

GRAPHICS
Flat artwork prepared for filming under an animation stand. Typical graphic ELEMENTS are titles, lettering and logos.

GRAPHICS ANIMATION
The animation of two-dimensional graphic images.

GRAPHICS TABLET
See DIGITIZING TABLE/TABLET.

GRAY CARD
An even mid tone gray card used to evaluate proper exposure. A gray card represents 18% reflectance of the light striking it and is often placed at the head of a roll of film as a control device to help determine how bright a scene should be printed.

GRAY SCALE
A chart of several incremental gray images ranging from black to white. Such a scale is generally used in conjunction with a GRAY CARD in determining how to properly expose or print a scene.

GREEN RECORD
See COLOR SEPARATIONS.

GREEN SCREEN
A large green backing against which a subject is photo
graphed in LIMBO. Identical in use to the BLUESCREEN
green screens are generally front lit for use primarily in videc
effects.

GRID
A pattern of vertical and horizontal lines used to positior
images within the frame. See FIELD CHART.

HALF–SILVERED MIRROR
See FIFTY–FIFTY MIRROR.

HANDLES
Extra frames of film at the HEAD and TAIL of the EXAC
CUT of an effects shot which are included in a COMPOSITI
as a safety measure should the exact cut change.

HANGING MINIATURE SHOT
A special effects technique which serves a similar purpose a
a GLASS SHOT, except rather than placing a sheet of glas
between the lens and subject, an actual miniature is posi
tioned in front of the camera. The miniature is sometime
specially built to blend into some feature in the BACK
GROUND of the scene.

HARD COPY
Images or information which can be viewed without usin
an intermediate device such as a MONITOR, for example
paper print–out of computer data or an image on film
"Hard" implies a non–volatile copy which can be handled
See SOFT COPY.

HARD DISC
A metal disc coated with magnetic material used for the mas
storage of computer data. Also called HARD DISC DRIVE

HARD DISC DRIVE
See HARD DISC.

HARD EDGED MATTE
A MATTE with edges which are sharp and well defined as opposed to a SOFT EDGED MATTE with edges which are softly graduated.

HARDWARE
Any machine or equipment used for film, video or computing processes as distinguished from SOFTWARE, which includes such items as computer programs and videotape.

HARRY™
A DIGITAL VIDEO EFFECTS DEVICE used for video editing and compositing.

HCORP
An abbreviation for HOT COLOR REGISTERED PRINT.

HDTV
Abbreviation for HIGH DEFINITION TELEVISION. See HIGH DEFINITION TELEVISION.

HEAD(S)
The beginning of a roll of film.

HELD FRAME
See FREEZE FRAME.

HI CON
An abbreviation for HIGH CONTRAST FILM.

HIDDEN SURFACES
Those surfaces on a fully RENDERED COMPUTER GENERATED IMAGE which are not visible behind foreground surfaces.

HIGH CONTRAST FILM
A film EMULSION which is capable of recording the extremes of light and dark with very few gray values in between. High contrast film emulsions are useful in certain MATTING applications.

HIGH DEFINITION MONITOR
A video monitor which DISPLAYS an image of higher resolution than the standard 525 lines. High definition monitors

are essential when working with HIGH RESOLUTION DIGITAL IMAGEs.

HIGH DEFINITION TELEVISION
A television system based on higher picture resolution than the standard 525 lines. Several systems differing in resolution are currently in development by competing companies, but the high definition standard seems to be heading toward 1125 lines.

HIGH DEFINITION VIDEO
See HIGH DEFINITION TELEVISION.

HIGH PASS FILTER
A filtering process used in COMPUTER GRAPHICS to sharpen an image and improve detail.

HI RES
See HIGH RESOLUTION IMAGE.

HIGH RESOLUTION IMAGE
Reference made to a DIGITAL IMAGE of sufficient resolution to be output onto film. Most digital image manipulation is done at LOW RESOLUTION which is much faster to compute. Only the final calculations are executed at high resolution.

HIGH RESOLUTION MONITOR
See HIGH DEFINITION MONITOR.

HIGH RESOLUTION TELEVISION
See HIGH DEFINITION TELEVISION.

HIGH RESOLUTION VIDEO
See HIGH DEFINITION VIDEO.

HIGH SPEED CAMERA
Any camera which can film at a rate in excess of normal sound speed of 24 frames per second.

HIGH SPEED PHOTOGRAPHY
Any photographic process which involves filming at frame rates in excess of 24 frames per second. Typical high speed applications are explosions, crashes and slow motion effects.

HISTOGRAM
A plotted graph which displays the count of PIXELS which share a common set of ATTRIBUTES, such as color or VALUE.

HOLD BACK MATTE
See FEMALE MATTE and BLUESCREEN PROCESS.

HOLD FRAME
See FREEZE FRAME.

HOLD OUT MATTE
See MALE MATTE and BLUESCREEN PROCESS.

HOLOGRAM
A three dimensional image created with holography.

HOLOGRAPHY
The process of creating a three dimensional image on a flat piece of film with the use of laser light.

HOT
A general reference to an image which is too bright, e.g., "The image is too hot."

HOT COLOR REGISTERED PRINT
An overexposed color print made on an OPTICAL PRINTER onto ESTAR BASED stock. These REGISTERED PRINTS are necessary when performing critical lineup or rotoscope operations where the image must be steady and clearly visible.

HOT HEAD™
A remote controlled camera gear head.

HOT SPLICE
An overlapping cemented film splice in which the cement is heated for quick drying.

HUE
A specific color in the color spectrum.

HUE CIRCLE
A display of all the colors of the spectrum ranging from red to orange to yellow to green to blue to violet and back to red again.
(See illustration on page 92.)

HYPERSPACE
A term lifted from the "Star Wars" trilogy which describes the effect of light streaking past camera as if traveling through outer space at the speed of light.

I

ICON
A picture symbol used in many computer programs to represent a command, operation or tool to be selected by the user.

ILM
Abbreviation for Industrial Light and Magic, a special effects company formed by George Lucas to create the special effects for Star Wars.

IMAGE ENHANCEMENT
The use of a computer to improve the quality of an image by removing noise or by increasing CONTRAST or sharpness in order to reveal detail which otherwise might be difficult to see.

IMAGE MAPPING
The process of placing an image over a three-dimensional form within a computer in much the same way as a slip cover is placed over furniture. The shape of the original form is retained but the surface has the ATTRIBUTES of the mapped image. See REFLECTION MAPPING and TEXTURE MAPPING.

IMAGE MEMORY
See BITMAP.

IMAGE PROCESSING
The enhancement or manipulation of DIGITAL IMAGES by a computer. See COMPUTER GRAPHICS.

IMAGE SYNTHESIS
The creation of an image with the use of a computer.

IMAGE WARPING
The IMAGE PROCESSING technique of altering an image by distorting or "warping" the original image. Such warping is often used to transform one image into another during a TRANSFORMATION EFFECT.

IMAX™
A photographic and exhibition system which uses 65 mm film traveling horizontally through the camera to achieve the largest film frame in motion picture history. IMAX, which differs from OMNIMAX in that it is projected on a flat screen,

is primarily used for specialty films which are shown at theme parks throughout the world. See FORMAT.

IN BETWEEN ANIMATION
The animated drawings which complete an action determined by KEY FRAMES.

IN BETWEENS
See IN BETWEEN ANIMATION.

IN CAMERA
See IN CAMERA EFFECTS.

IN CAMERA EFFECTS
Visual effects which are achieved using single or multiple passes through a single camera, as opposed to those created by the COMPOSITE of multiple ELEMENTS.

IN CAMERA MATTE SHOT
See LATENT IMAGE MATTE SHOT.

INCIDENT LIGHT METER
An instrument which reads the amount of the light falling on a subject. See also REFLECTIVE LIGHT METER .

INK AND PAINT
The process of tracing with ink onto clear acetate cels the line drawings made by an animator. These ink drawings are then painted with the details of the subject in preparation for filming.

INKER
The person who performs the function of tracing over a pencil drawing with ink.

INKING
1) The process of tracing over pencil drawings with ink.
2) A process in which holes in a MATTE are filled in by hand using ink. Also called OPAQUING.

INPUT DEVICE
Any device used to convert non–digital images such as photographs or artwork into DIGITAL IMAGES. The process involves dividing the image into thousands of tiny dots called PIXELS (PICTURE ELEMENTS), and assigning numbers which correspond to the color and brightness of each point. See DIGITIZE.

INPUT SCANNER
A device used to convert a film image into DIGITAL information which a computer can then manipulate. The process involves dividing the frame into thousands of tiny dots called PIXELS (PICTURE ELEMENTS), and assigning numbers which correspond tothe color and brightness of each point. See DIGITIZE.

INTEGRATED CIRCUIT
Proper name for "CHIP." See COMPUTER CHIP.

INTERACTIVE
A machine or process which provides REAL TIME response or feedback to the user.

INTERACTIVE LIGHT ANIMATION
Animation which creates the effect of highlights on objects within a scene caused by a light effect added in post production.

INTERLACING
The process by which alternate fields of a video image are displayed by the scanning electron beam. First the odd numbered lines are scanned, then the even numbered lines, thereby reducing image FLICKER.

INTERLOCK
The process of electronically synchronizing two or more motors, such as projector motors during screening of dailies with separate picture and sound reels.

INTER MATTE
Abbreviation for INTERMEDIATE MATTE.

INTERMEDIATE COMPOSITING ELEMENTS
See INTERMEDIATE ELEMENT.

INTERMEDIATE ELEMENT
Any of many images made from the CAMERA ORIGINAL of a scene ELEMENT which aid in the compositing process. Intermediate elements include INTERMEDIATE POSITIVE, BLUE PRINT, COLOR SEPARATIONS, MATTES, etc.

INTERMEDIATE MATTE
A MATTE which is used as an intermediate step in creating another. See BLUESCREEN PROCESS.

INTERMEDIATE NEGATIVE
A reversal print of an ORIGINAL NEGATIVE from which prints could then be made without risking damage to the ORIGINAL. Also called INTERNEG.

INTERMEDIATE POSITIVE
An POSITIVE image made from an ORIGINAL NEGATIVE which is then used as an ELEMENT during a COMPOSITE. Typically BACKGROUND elements are composited into a shot from an intermediate positive, or "IP." Also called INTERPOSITIVE.

INTERMITTENT PRINTER
A printer which firmly registers each frame of film to be duplicated onto REGISTRATION PINS prior to exposure. This type of printer is the workhorse of OPTICAL PRINTING and is distinguished from a continuous printer which offers no REGISTRATION of the image.

INTERNEG
Abbreviation for INTERMEDIATE NEGATIVE.

INTERNEGATIVE
Abbreviation for INTERMEDIATE NEGATIVE.

INTERPOS
An abbreviation for INTERMEDIATE POSITIVE.

INTERPOSITIVE
Abbreviation for INTERMEDIATE POSITIVE.

INTERVALOMETER
A camera control device which allows the exposure of film frames at predetermined intervals.

IN THE CAN
A finished project is said to be "in the can." The term is derived from the fact that a finished release print of a film is packaged in "cans" for shipment to the theaters.

INTROVISION™
A FRONT PROJECTION PROCESS which uses a secondary screen and special lenses to allow actors to appear from behind doorways or other objects in the BACKGROUND projection plate.

IP
An abbreviation for INTERMEDIATE POSITIVE.

IRIS
The diaphragm inside a lens which opens and closes to regulate the amount of light which reaches the film plane.

J

JAGGIES
See ALIASING.

JOYSTICK
Any of a variety of input devices used with MOTION CONTROL systems. A typical joystick consists of a metal box which houses some electronic components, and a dial of some sort which controls the speed of a motor.

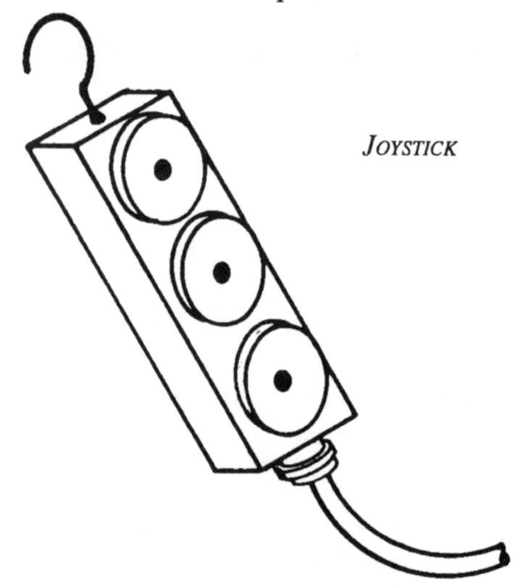

JOYSTICK

JUMP OUT
See SKIP OUT.

KEY
An electronic method of MATTING one image over another by "cutting" a black hole into the first image and filling the hole with a second image. The process is somewhat like using a cookie cutter on freshly rolled dough.

KEY ANIMATOR
The person responsible for designing the motion or action of an animated character or effect.

KEYBOARD
A typewriter–like set of keys used to enter text and numbers into a computer.

KEY FRAME ANIMATION
Animation which determines the major poses to be struck by an animated character or effect. IN BETWEEN drawings then complete the action for a smooth motion.

KEY FRAMES
Those moments within a shot which determine critical composition, position or motion of ELEMENTS. In certain applications of MOTION CONTROL programming, the subject and camera are set at strategic key positions while the computer automatically interpolates the various positions in between.

KEY NUMBERS
See EDGE NUMBERS.

KEY POINTS
Those points along a curve which approximate the overall shape of the curve when connected by straight lines.

KEYSTONE DISTORTION
The tendency of wide angle lenses to distort images at the right and left edges of the frame. The selection of wide angle lenses must usually be avoided for this reason when shooting ELEMENTS to be inserted into the body of a larger scene.
(See illustration on page 72.)

KEYSTONING
See KEYSTONE DISTORTION.

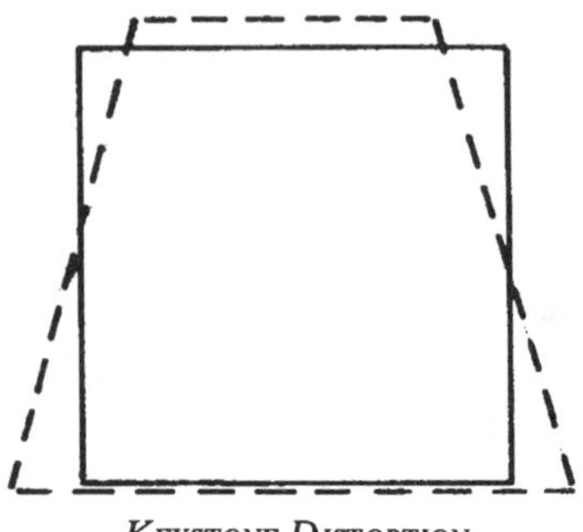

Keystone Distortion

KODAK GIRL
See GIRL HEAD.

KODAK STANDARD PERFORATION
The rectangular perforation with rounded corners which is standard on all print stock in the United States.
(See PERFORATION illustration on page 108.)

KODALITH
Extremely high CONTRAST sheet film used in special effects animation. Kodaliths are commonly used as artwork for BURN IN titles.

L

LAB ROLL
Large rolls of film assembled at a lab from smaller rolls of customer negative. Lab rolls are created to cut down on the handling of each piece of negative during lab operations.

LAP DISSOLVE
See CROSS DISSOLVE.

LARGE FORMAT CAMERA
A still camera which uses large negatives (e.g., 4″ x 5″ or 8″x 10.″) The images produced by these cameras are often used for front or rear projection plates of non–moving backgrounds.

LASER
An acronym for *Light Amplification by Simulated Emission of Radiation.* A device which amplifies and concentrates light of

a particular wavelength into an intense and narrow beam. Lasers are used in film– making to create a host of interesting REAL TIME light effects.

LASER DISC
See OPTICAL DISC.

LASER PRINTER
An OUTPUT DEVICE which uses a laser beam to convert DIGITAL IMAGES into film images. Also refers to common high quality desktop computer printers.

LASER SCANNER
An INPUT SCANNER which uses a laser beam to read the color and brightness of each of several thousand points within a film image. See INPUT SCANNER.

LATENT IMAGE
An image which has been exposed onto a piece of negative but which has not yet been developed.

LATENT IMAGE MATTE SHOT
A MATTE PAINTING technique in which a live action scene is photographed with a portion blacked out by a piece of painted glass which has been placed in front of the lens. The film is not processed until the blackened portion of the image is filled in with an exposure to a MATTE PAINTING. Latent image matte

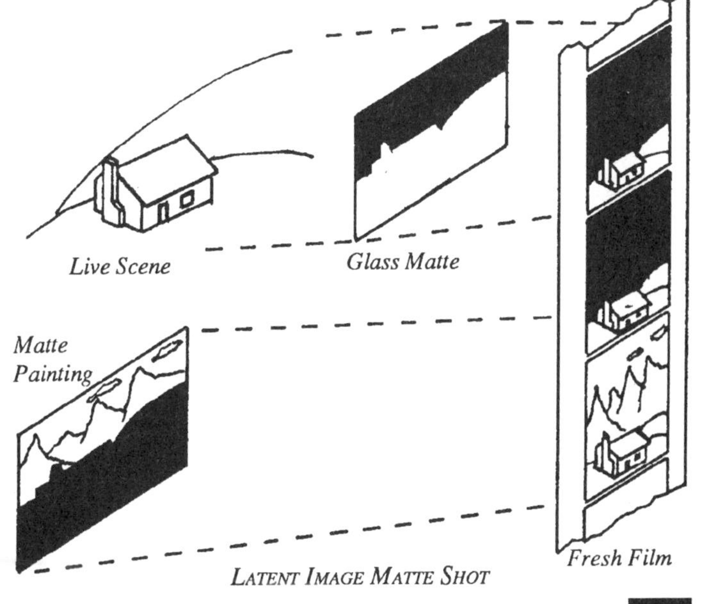

LATENT IMAGE MATTE SHOT

shots have the advantage of yielding a first generation COMPOSITE negative as opposed to the second generation negative produced by traditional OPTICAL COMPOSITING.

LATENT IMAGE MATTING
See LATENT IMAGE MATTE SHOT.

LATITUDE
The ability of a particular film stock to tolerate improper exposure while delivering an acceptable image.

LENS BELLOWS
See BELLOWS ATTACHMENT.

LIGHT BOX
A table or box with a white plexiglas top which is lit from underneath to produce an even light source for viewing film clips or animation drawings.

LIGHT PASS
An auxiliary pass to the BEAUTY PASS which normally involves long exposure times to record PRACTICAL lights on a model or miniature set. See PASS.

LIGHT PEN
A light sensitive STYLUS which is used to draw images or select menu items by touching the screen of a CRT. The light pen sends a pulse back to the computer when struck by the scanning electron beam, thus locating the pen on the screen.

LIGHT TABLE
A table which has a LIGHT BOX recessed into the top.

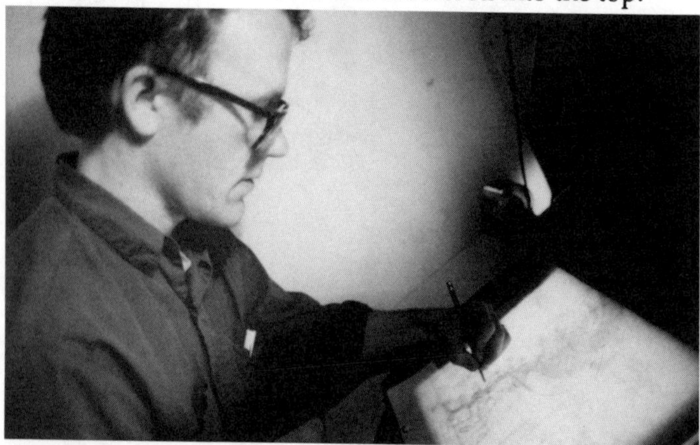

Animator John Armstrong works at a LIGHT TABLE. Photo courtesy Lucasfilm Ltd.

LIGHT VALUE
The degree of brightness or darkness of an image.

LIMBO
The state of being surrounded by a background devoid of details, such as with a BLUESCREEN or black BACKING.

LIMITED ANIMATION
A low budget animation technique in which most parts of an animated figure are held stationary while moving just a few, such as the lips and eyes.

LINE TEST
See PENCIL TEST.

LINEUP
The process of physically organizing and preparing the various pieces of film which make up an OPTICAL COMPOSITE.

LINEUP PERSON
The person responsible for physically organizing the various ELEMENTS which make up a OPTICAL COMPOSITE. He or she ensures that all required elements are present and generates instructions for the OPTICAL PRINTER operator.

LINEUP SHEET
The list of instructions to the OPTICAL PRINTER operator which the LINEUP PERSON creates. This sheet contains all information pertinent to filming the COMPOSITE, including exposure and color correction information, special filtration requirements and counts as to which images are to be combined on each frame of the composite.

LIQUID GATE
See WET GATE PRINTING.

LIQUID GATE PRINTING
See WET GATE PRINTING.

LIVE ACTION
Generally refers to any scene which is not a special visual effect, while specifically referring to the principal photography of the movie.

LIVE ACTION MOTION CONTROL
See REAL TIME MOTION CONTROL.

LIVE ACTION PLATE
A scene filmed in conjunction with the first or second units of a motion picture which is intended to be the basis of a special visual effects shot. See also BACKGROUND PLATE.

LOCKED OFF
A camera that makes no move during a scene is said to be "locked off."

LO CON
Abbreviation for LOW CONTRAST print. Low contrast prints are used whenever a POSITIVE is to be rephotographed, such as with a PIN BLOCK unit.

LOOK–UP TABLE
A table of information used by a computer to adjust color and brightness of an image as it is delivered to an output device.

LOOP PRINTING
The process of printing a set number of frames over and over again with the action proceeding in the same direction.

LOOP TREE
A device which holds a loop of film while it is being projected for repeated viewing.

LOW CONTRAST FILM
A film EMULSION which is chemically balanced to produce an image which is of lower than normal CONTRAST.

LOW CONTRAST FILTER
A photographic filter used to slightly reduce the CONTRAST in a scene to be filmed.

LOW PASS FILTER
A filtering process in COMPUTER GRAPHICS in which an image is softened by averaging each PIXEL with its eight neighbors to create a new pixel. The process has much the same effect as a DIFFUSION FILTER in front of a camera lens.

LOW RES
See LOW RESOLUTION IMAGE.

LOW RESOLUTION IMAGE
Reference made to a DIGITAL IMAGE of insufficient resolution for final output onto film. Low resolution images are much quicker to compute and manipulate than HIGH RESO-

LUTION IMAGES. For this reason most DIGITAL "works in progress" use low resolution pictures with only the final calculations being executed in HIGH RESOLUTION.

LOW SPEED CAMERA
A camera designed to film at frame rates below the standard sound speed rate of 24 frames per second. Low speed cameras are used for MOTION CONTROL PHOTOGRAPHY, TIME LAPSE PHOTOGRAPHY, ANIMATION and STOP MOTION PHOTOGRAPHY and many other special effects techniques.

LUPE
A special viewing glass designed for looking at a single frame of film over a LIGHT BOX.

LUSTRE
The property of the surface of an object which determines how reflective it will be.

MACHINE CODE
See MACHINE LANGUAGE.

MACHINE LANGUAGE
Computer programming language in the form of BINARY DIGITS which are immediately understood by a computer without translation. Higher level languages such as Basic and Fortran must be converted to machine language before they are understood by a computer.

MACRO LENS
A lens used in close up photography which is capable of very close focusing.

MACRO PHOTOGRAPHY
Close up photography using special lenses and lens extenders.

MAGAZINE
See FILM MAGAZINE.

MAGENTA
One of the SUBTRACTIVE COLORS of light used in OPTICAL PRINTING. Magenta light is produced by subtracting the PRIMARY COLOR green from white light. Adding magenta to a scene is equivalent to removing green. See COLOR TRIANGLE.

MAGNETIC TAPE DEVICE
A bulk storage device used to hold massive data FILES of no immediate use to the computer.

MAINFRAME
A powerful central computer which serves as a host to several terminals or auxiliary computers, disc drives, printers, etc.

MAKEUP APPLIANCE
See PROSTHETIC MAKEUP APPLIANCE.

MAKEUP EFFECTS
A transformation of a human face to another character using prosthetic and traditional makeup techniques.

MALE MATTE
A MATTE used in OPTICAL PRINTING which features the black silhouette of a foreground subject against a clear field. Also commonly referred to as a HOLDOUT MATTE, BLACK CORE MATTE or BLACK CENTER MATTE, it is principally used to create a black "hole" in a BACKGROUND into which the foreground subject is then printed. See BLUESCREEN PROCESS.

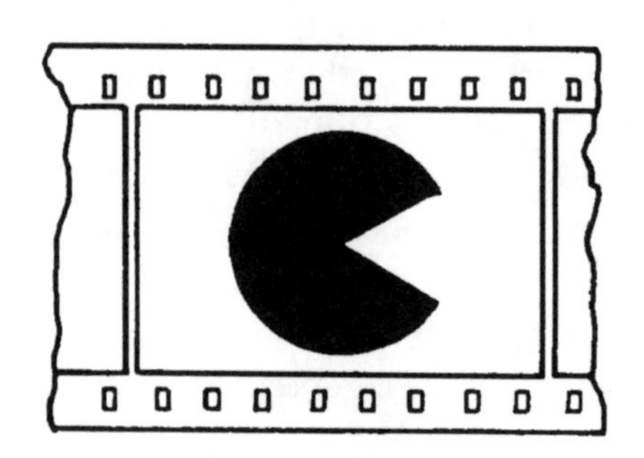

Male Matte

MAPPING
See IMAGE MAPPING.

MARIONETTE RIG
A device to which a model is connected by thin wires in such a way that when the rig moves, the model moves in the same manner. Marionette rigs are used to suspend models into a shot while keeping the model mover equipment out of frame.

MARIONETTE RIG used during the filming of model sequences of "Batteries Not Included." Photo courtesy Lucasfilm Ltd.

MARKER
See CLAPSTICKS.

MASK
1) A MATTE placed in front of a taking camera to partially obscure or reshape the frame. Such masks could be used to simulate the view through a pair of binoculars or a keyhole.

(See illustration on page 80.)

2) A series of metal plates which are inserted into the gate of a projector to change the projected image from one ASPECT RATIO to another.

MASKED PRINT
A specially generated print which has extremely low CONTRAST.

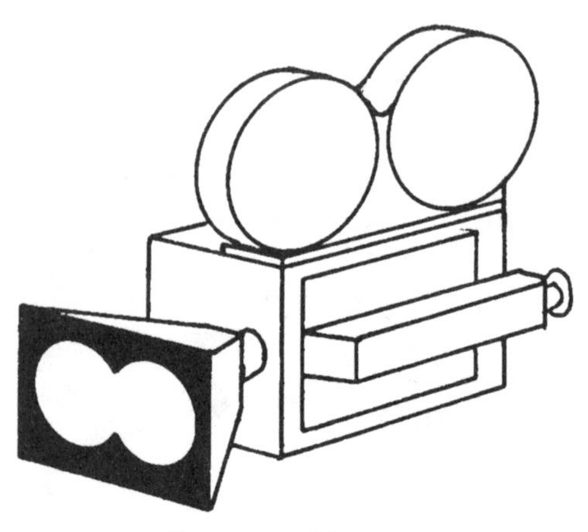

Binoculars Mask

MASTER
The original recording, either video or audio, from which copies are made.

MASTER MOTOR
An encoded motor which is used to remotely drive a SLAVE MOTOR. This dual motor concept is the basis for many remote control camera systems such as the popular Hot Head.

MATCHED MOVE
When two ELEMENTS of a shot have the exact same camera move built into them, the moves are said to be "matched." Matched moves are usually accomplished with the help of a MOTION CONTROL system, but at times they are generated by PLOTTING an existing move under an animation stand.

MATCHED MOVE PHOTOGRAPHY
The process of photographing additional ELEMENTS for a scene with a camera move which has been created by PLOTTING the camera movement in a BACKGROUND PLATE. The recent advent of REAL TIME MOTION CONTROL systems has eliminated much of the need for plotting to achieve matched move elements.

MATTE
Any opaque or semi–opaque image whose principal function is to prevent the exposure of an area of film. See BLUESCREEN PHOTOGRAPHY.

MATTE, ARTICULATE
See ARTICULATE MATTE.

MATTE, BLACK CENTER
See MALE MATTE.

MATTE, BLACK CORE
See MALE MATTE.

MATTE, BLUE SPILL
See BLUE SPILL MATTE.

MATTE, BURN–IN
See FEMALE MATTE.

MATTE, CLEAR CENTER
See FEMALE MATTE.

MATTE, CLEAR CORE
See FEMALE MATTE.

MATTE, COUNTER
See COMPLEMENTARY MATTE.

MATTE, COVER
See FEMALE MATTE.

MATTE, DIFFERENCE
See DIFFERENCE MATTE.

MATTE, FEMALE
See FEMALE MATTE.

MATTE, GARBAGE
See GARBAGE MATTE.

MATTE, HAND DRAWN
See ROTOSCOPED MATTE.

MATTE, HARD EDGED
See HARD EDGED MATTE.

MATTE, HOLD BACK
See FEMALE MATTE.

MATTE, HOLD OUT
See MALE MATTE.

MATTE, INTER
See INTERMEDIATE MATTE.

MATTE, MALE
See MALE MATTE.

MATTE, ROD ARTICULATE
See ROD ARTICULATE MATTE.

MATTE, ROTO
See ROTOSCOPED MATTE.

MATTE, ROTOSCOPED
See ROTOSCOPED MATTE.

MATTE, SOFT EDGED
See SOFT EDGED MATTE.

MATTE, SPILL
See BLUE SPILL MATTE.

MATTE, SPLIT
See SPLIT MATTE

MATTE, TRAVELING
See TRAVELING MATTE and BLUESCREEN PROCESS.

MATTE, WIPE
See REVEAL MATTE.

MATTE ARTIST
The artist who creates MATTE PAINTINGS.

MATTE BOX
A small semi–enclosed device fixed in front of a camera lens into which filters and masks can be placed.

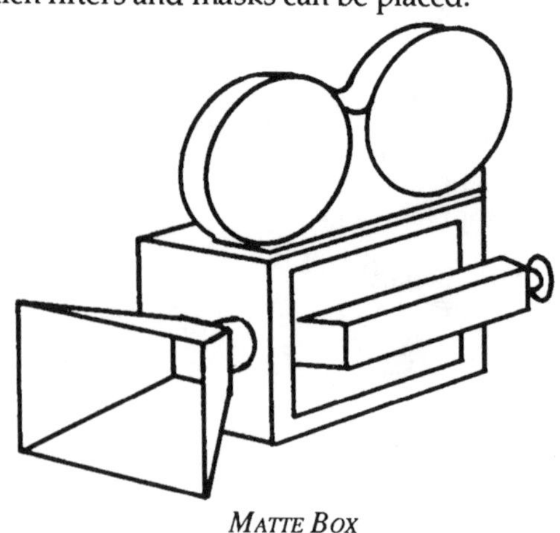

MATTE BOX

MATTE FIT
The proper positioning of male and female mattes during a COMPOSITE in order to eliminate visible MATTE LINES.

MATTE LINE
A black or white line visible along the edges of an object which has been improperly matted into a scene.

MATTE PAINTER
See MATTE ARTIST.

MATTE PAINTING
A painting, usually on glass, which augments or replaces a live action image. Matte paintings are used to create fantasy environments or add scope or complexity to a shot which would be too expensive or impossible to film for real.
(See color photographs on page 94.)

MATTE PASS
An auxiliary pass to the BEAUTY PASS in which a subject is silhouetted against a white card or back light source. The resultant image can be used as a MATTE for compositing. See PASS.

MATTE SHOT
A special effects shot which employs a MATTE PAINTING.

MATTE STEADY PLATFORM
A platform or tower which is rigid enough to be used as a camera position for a MATTE SHOT.

MATTE TRANSPARENCY
See TRANSPARENCY.

MATTING
Any process in which two or more separate images are combined with the use of MATTES to prevent the SUPERIMPOSITION of those images.

MECHANICAL EFFECTS
Special effects which are performed at the time of principal photography without the use of photographic tricks. For example: robotics, rock slides, collapsing walls, explosions, bullet hits, flood effects, rain, snow, etc.

MEG
Abbreviation for MEGABYTE, one million bytes.

MENU
A list displayed on a computer screen which offers a series of options or COMMANDS available to the user.

MENU BAR
A strip containing MENU items which resides along the top of a computer screen.

MENU DRIVEN
A computer program in which the user issues commands and makes choices by selecting from a series of predetermined menu items as opposed to typing commands on the keyboard.

MESH WARP
A technique of IMAGE WARPING which begins with the temporary superimposition of a grid or "mesh" over an image. Each square of the grid can then be individually distorted by moving the various intersecting points to slightly new positions. The distortion apparent in the mesh is then transferred to the underlying image. Mesh warping can be used to create TRANSFORMATION EFFECTS.

MIDDLE GROUND
In COMPOSITE PHOTOGRAPHY, an ELEMENT which crosses over the BACKGROUND, but which itself is crossed over by a foreground element, is said to be in the "middle ground."

MINIATURE
A replica of a person, setting, or object in any scale smaller than real life.

MINIATURE REAR PROJECTION
A rear projection technique in which a life size scene is reduced and inserted into a miniature set.

MINIATURE SHOT
Any shot which uses a miniature as a principal component.

MIRAGE™
A DIGITAL VIDEO EFFECTS device manufactured by Quantel which allows for the three dimensional manipulation of images.

MIRROR IMAGE
The new image created when the right and left hand polarities are reversed, as though you were looking into a mirror.
(See illustration on page 85.)

MODEL
Any replica or likeness of a person, setting or object, either real or imaginary, as in a mathematical description inside a computer.

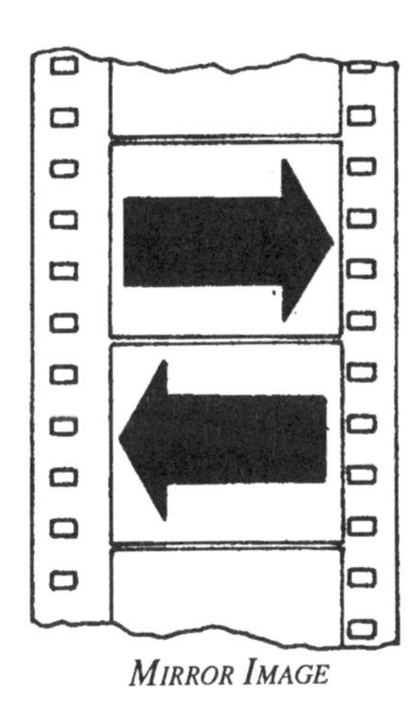

MIRROR IMAGE

MODELING
The COMPUTER GRAPHICS process of adding surface detail to a DIGITAL IMAGE. Modeling an image includes adding color, lighting and texture detail.

MODELING AN IMAGE
See MODELING.

MODEL MAKER
A person who makes models.

MODEL MOVER
A computer controlled mechanical apparatus onto which a model is mounted to be moved during a shot.

MODEL SHOT
Any shot which uses a model as a principal component.

MODEM
Contraction of MODULATOR–DEMODULATOR. A device which allows for the transfer of data between computers over normal telephone lines. A sending modem converts DIGITAL information into electrical pulses while the receiving modem converts the pulses back to DIGITAL form.

MOIRE EFFECT
An animation effect created by moving two geometrical patterns, such as lines or arcs, over one another.
(See illustration on page 86.)

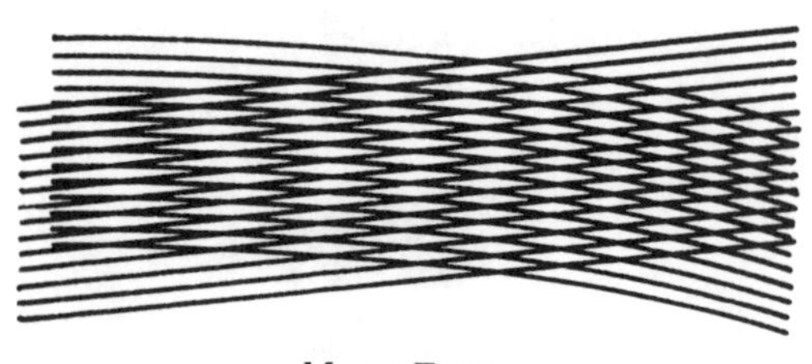

MOIRE EFFECT

MOLE FAN™
Trademarked name for a compact yet powerful fan manufactured by Mole Richardson used to create small scale wind effects.

MOLE SMOKER™
Trademarked name for a smoke generator manufactured by Mole Richardson.

MONITOR
A professional grade of the standard television receiver which may or may not include a tuner or sound system. Monitors are available at RESOLUTION in excess of the standard 525 lines.

MORPH
See MORPHING.

MORPHING
The IMAGE PROCESSING technique of transforming one image into another by progressively altering the size, shape, color and texture of the original imagery. The name derives from "metamorphosis" and is also commonly referred to as a MORPH.
(See color photographs on page 95.)

MOTION BLUR
The natural occurrence of blur in an image as the subject moves through the frame during exposure. The amount of motion blur increases as the speed of the subject or the exposure time increases.

MOTION CONTROL
Any computer–based command center designed to control an endless variety of hardware in order to repeatedly execute a pre–programmed camera or subject move. Motion control systems are a common operating feature on TRACK and ANIMATION CAMERAS, as well as OPTICAL PRINTERS. Motion control systems are the foundation of many visual effects techniques and are infinitely adaptable to special needs.

MOTION CONTROL ANIMATION STAND
An ANIMATION STAND with all axes of movement and camera function controlled by a MOTION CONTROL system.

MOTION CONTROL OPTICAL PRINTER
An OPTICAL PRINTER with all axes of movement and camera/projector function controlled by a MOTION CONTROL system.

MOTION CONTROL SYSTEM
Any camera, projection or other electro–mechanical apparatus which uses computers to record and playback motion.

MOTION CONTROL SYSTEM composed of a custom computer and camera apparatus. Photo courtesy Lucasfilm Ltd.

MOTION GRAPHICS
See GRAPHICS ANIMATION.

MOTION TEST
See PENCIL TEST.

MOUSE
A hand–held device used by many SOFTWARE and computer systems to position the CURSER on a COMPUTER SCREEN. A small ball exposed on the underside of the mouse rolls when the mouse is moved along a flat surface. The computer uses the rolling ball to track the position of the mouse, which then translates to the position of the curser on the screen.

MOVEMENT
See CAMERA MOVEMENT.

Photo Captions

From Top to Bottom on page 89:

A. *AERIAL PERSPECTIVE is well illustrated in this MATTE PAINTING scene from "Willow."*
"Willow" ™ & © Lucasfilm Ltd. (LFL) 1988. All Rights Reserved.

B. *A painted BACKING was used in this scene from "The Empire Strikes Back."*
"Empire" ™ & © Lucasfilm Ltd. (LFL) 1980. All Rights Reserved.

From Top to Bottom on page 90:

BLUESCREEN PROCESS:

In this typical bluescreen composite from "Return of the Jedi," we have:

A. *The BACKGROUND PLATE*
"Jedi" ™ & © Lucasfilm Ltd. (LFL) 1980. All Rights Reserved.

B. *The BLUESCREEN PLATE*
"Jedi" ™ & © Lucasfilm Ltd. (LFL) 1980. All Rights Reserved.

C. *A ROD ARTICULATE MATTE used to eliminate the mounting rod of the speeder bike.*
"Jedi" ™ & © Lucasfilm Ltd. (LFL) 1980. All Rights Reserved.

D. *GARBAGE MATTE used to eliminate all other undesired imagery.*
"Jedi" ™ & © Lucasfilm Ltd. (LFL) 1980. All Rights Reserved.

From Top to Bottom on page 91:

BLUESCREEN PROCESS continued:

E. *The FEMALE MATTE with use of both the rod articulate and garbage matte.*
"Jedi" ™ & © Lucasfilm Ltd. (LFL) 1982. All Rights Reserved.

F. *The MALE MATTE, a PRINTBACK of the female matte.*
"Jedi" ™ & © Lucasfilm Ltd. (LFL) 1982. All Rights Reserved.

G. *The background with a black hole created by using the male matte to block exposure over the area to be occupied by the speeder bike.*
"Jedi" ™ & © Lucasfilm Ltd. (LFL) 1982. All Rights Reserved.

H. *The final composite. The speeder bike is exposed into the scene through the female matte, which prevents contamination of the background from the bluescreen.*
"Jedi" ™ & © Lucasfilm Ltd. (LFL) 1982. All Rights Reserved.

All photographs courtesy Lucasfilm Ltd.

A.

B.

A.

B.

C.

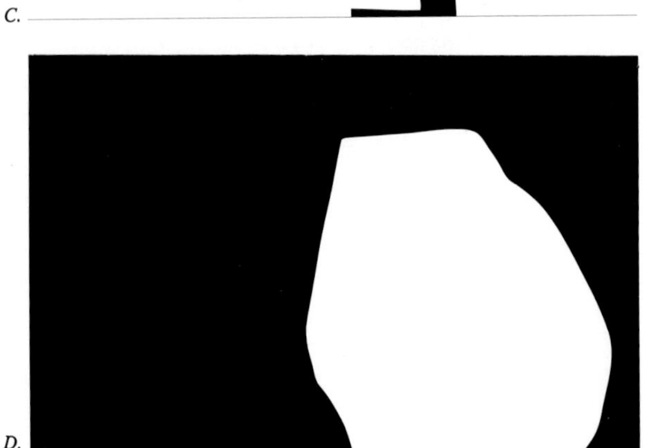

D.

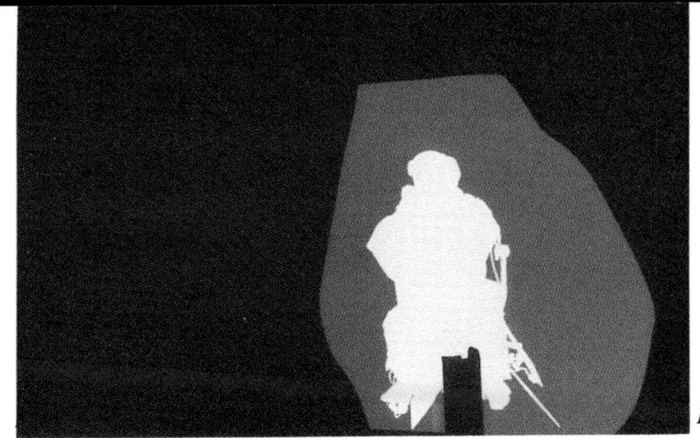

E.

F.

G.

H.

Additive colors

A.

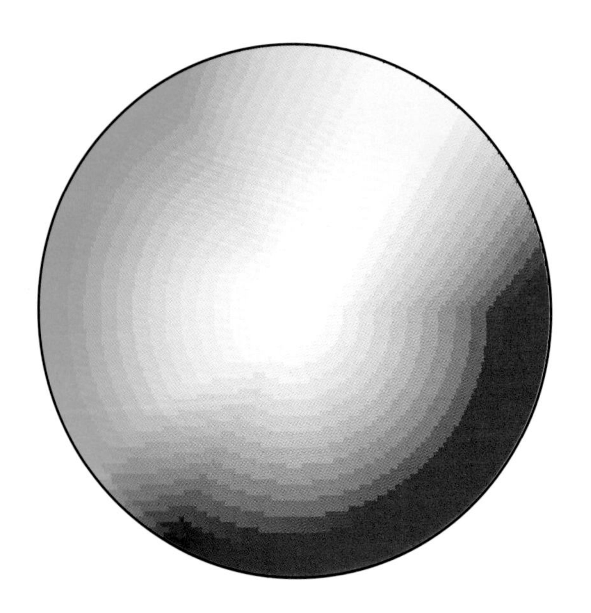

B.

Hue Circle

A.

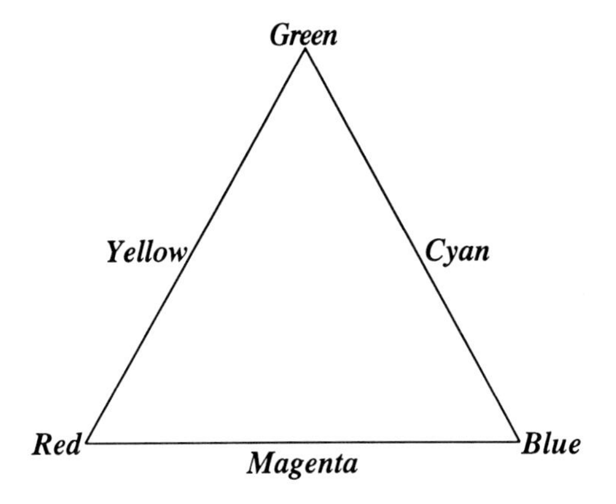

B.

COLOR TRIANGLE

A.

B.

C.

A.

B.

C.

Photo Captions

From top to bottom on page 92:

A. *ADDITIVE COLORS*

B. *HUE CIRCLE*

From top to bottom on page 93:

C. *SUBTRACTIVE COLORS*

D. *COLOR TRIANGLE*

From top to bottom on page 94:

A. *ROD PUPPET characters which appeared in the film, "Young Sherlock Holmes." Photo courtesy Lucasfilm Ltd.*

B-C *Famous MATTE PAINTING from "Raiders of the Lost Ark." Only the small area surrounding the warehouse worker in the scene was real.*

From top to bottom on page 95:

A-C *This MORPH scene from "Willow" changed a tiger into an old woman.*

All photographs on pages 94-95 courtesy Lucasfilm Ltd.

MOVIOLA
A trademarked portable film viewing device used primarily by film editors.

MULTI IMAGE
A technique which produces several distinct images on the screen at the same time.

MULTI FRAME PRINTING
See MULTIPLE PRINTING.

MULTIPLANE
A technique of animation which involves the positioning of two or more separate artworks on various levels beneath the camera. Each artwork can then be moved independently from the others to create parallactic movement, thereby simulating depth.

MULTIPLANE CAMERA
An ANIMATION STAND or TRACK CAMERA equipped to shoot multiplane effects. See MULTIPLANE.

MULTIPLE EXPOSURE
The process of making several exposures onto the same piece of film.

MULTIPLE PASS PHOTOGRAPHY
Any photographic process during which two or more exposures of the same subject are made. Each exposure, or PASS, can be made on a separate piece of film or as MULTIPLE EXPOSURES on the same piece of film. The latter case would be referred to as an IN–CAMERA EFFECT.

MULTIPLE PRINTING
The process of printing each frame of a moving picture more than once. This has the effect of slowing down the action in a staccato fashion.

ND
Abbreviation for NEUTRAL DENSITY.

ND FILTER
See NEUTRAL DENSITY FILTER.

NEGATIVE
The piece of film onto which a scene is first photographed. The light values of a negative image are reversed from the those of the original scene and the colors, if any, are complementary to those of the original scene. A negative is often called the CAMERA ORIGINAL.

NEGATIVE FILM
See NEGATIVE.

NEGATIVE FILM STOCK
See NEGATIVE.

NEGATIVE IMAGE
1) An image in which the LIGHT VALUES are reversed and the colors, if any, are COMPLEMENTARY to those in the original scene.
2) The image on a piece of negative film.

NEGATIVE PERFORATION
See BELL AND HOWELL STANDARD PERFORATION.

NEGATIVE PITCH
The distance between perforations measured along one side of a piece of negative, which is slightly shorter than that of a piece of positive film.
(See FRAME illustration on page 55.)

NEUTRAL DENSITY
The property of a photographic filter which causes all wavelengths of light to be absorbed equally, thus reducing the exposure without shifting the color of a scene. Abbreviated as ND.

NEUTRAL DENSITY FILTER
A filter which absorbs all wavelengths of light equally, thus reducing the exposure without shifting the apparent color of a scene. Abbreviated as ND FILTER.

NEWTON RINGS
A MOIRE PATTERN which sometimes appears in a COMPOSITE when two pieces of film in contact with each other are held in a freeze frame. They are caused by the diffraction of light at the point of contact between the two film surfaces.

NG

Abbreviation for "no good."

NIKONFLEX

A tiny STOP MOTION VISTAVISION camera which uses a Nikon still camera as the camera body and MOVEMENT. The Nikon body was modified to accept a specially built 50 foot FILM MAGAZINE while providing adequate REGISTRATION for non–composite miniature shots.

NIKONFLEX camera, complete with miniature pan and tilt head and dolly for use during the filming of the Mine Chase Sequence from "Indiana Jones and the Temple of Doom." Photo courtesy of Lucasfilm Ltd.

NINE TRACK TAPE

An off–line tape storage medium used in COMPUTER GRAPHICS to store up to 120 megabytes of data. In order for files stored on 9 track to be accessed by the computer, they must first be loaded onto disc. This storage medium is commonly used to store massive files that are not immediately required for processing by the computer. Also called MAGNETIC TAPE.

NODAL HEAD

A tripod head which allows the FRONT NODAL POINT of a lens to be positioned at one or more rotational axes of camera pan, tilt and roll.

NODAL POINT (FRONT NODAL POINT)

1) In a camera lens: the point inside the lens at which all light rays entering the lens seem to converge.
2) In a projector lens: the point inside the lens from which all light rays leaving the lens seem to emanate.

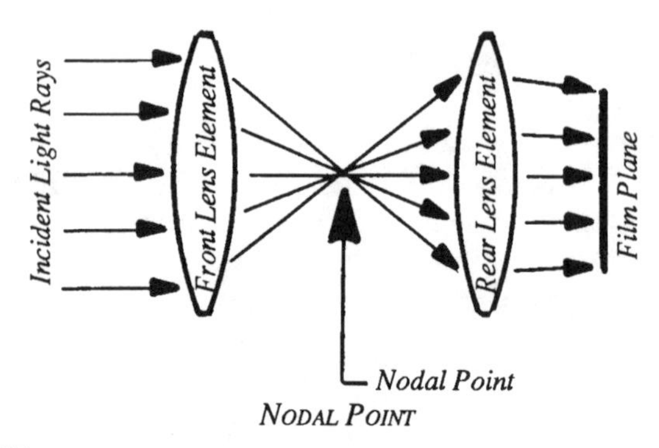

NODAL POINT

NOISE
Random electronic distortion in a video image which has the appearance of snow.

NORTH
A term borrowed from the compass referring to the top portion of an image or frame.

NTSC STANDARD
The United States video broadcast resolution standard of 525 lines.

NUMBER CRUNCHING
Computer slang for the process of executing a large number of calculations.

NYBBLE
Half a BYTE, or four BITS of computer information.

OBJECT ANIMATION
The simulation of movement of a three dimensional object by filming single frame images while incrementally displacing the object between frames. Such images, when projected at normal frame rates, create the illusion of movement. See STOP MOTION ANIMATION.

OFF–LINE
Equipment which is not directly communicating with a computer is said to be "off–line." OFF LINE EDITING refers to a lower cost process of cutting a video scene using equipment insufficient for broadcast quality. See also ON–LINE.

OFF–LINE EDITING
See OFF–LINE.

OMNIMAX™
A photographic and exhibition system which uses 65 mm film traveling horizontally through the camera to achieve the largest film frame in motion picture history. Omnimax, which is filmed through a fisheye lens and projected onto a curved screen, is primarily used for specialty films which are shown at theme parks throughout the world. See FORMAT and IMAX.

ONE LIGHT PRINT
A print made from a roll of negative with no attempt to COLOR TIME each scene. All scenes on the roll are printed with "one light."

ON–LINE
Equipment which is directly communicating with a computer is said to be "on–line." ON–LINE EDITING refers to the final step in video editing in which a high quality MASTER is edited in conformance to an OFF–LINE rough cut.

ON–LINE EDITING
See ON–LINE.

ON NODAL
A camera pan, tilt or roll move which pivots around the FRONT NODAL POINT of a lens is said to be "on nodal."

ON ONES/TWOS
Animation which utilizes a separate drawing for each frame of film is said to be "animated or shot on ones" as opposed to animation which utilizes one drawing for every two frames, which would be "animated or shot on twos." Animation on ones is of the highest quality, but also of the highest cost. Animation on twos is the quality standard for animated television shows for children, while nearly all animation for visual effects work is drawn on ones.

OPACITY
The opposite of TRANSPARENCY. The degree to which a film image blocks the transmission of light. A black image is of higher opacity than a gray image.

OPAQUING
The manual process of filling in the holes in a MATTE with ink or paint.

OPTICAL COMP
Abbreviation for OPTICAL COMPOSITE.

OPTICAL COMPOSITE (PHOTOGRAPHY)
The combining of two or more separate film images onto a third piece of RAWSTOCK with the use of an OPTICAL PRINTER.

OPTICAL DISC
Also called a LASER DISC. A specially treated plastic disc into which DIGITAL information is embedded by a LASER beam. For computer applications see CD–ROM.

OPTICAL EFFECTS
Visual effects which are traditionally achieved with the help of an OPTICAL PRINTER.

OPTICAL EFFECTS ANIMATION
The animation of images using an OPTICAL PRINTER.

OPTICAL FLIP
Using an OPTICAL PRINTER to invert an image so that top becomes bottom and vice versa. See also MIRROR IMAGE.

OPTICAL FLOP
See MIRROR IMAGE.

OPTICAL HOUSE
A facility which specializes in OPTICAL COMPOSITE PHOTOGRAPHY.

Optical Flip

OPTICAL LAYOUT
See LINEUP.

OPTICAL LINEUP
See LINEUP.

OPTICAL MOVE
A camera move across an image which is performed on an OPTICAL PRINTER.

OPTICAL PRINTER
A piece of equipment consisting of one or more projectors and lamp houses which project an image into the lens of a single taking camera for the purpose of duplicating film. Optical printers vary in complexity from a simple projector and camera used to convert film from one format to another, to very complex MOTION CONTROL printers in use at most modern OPTICAL HOUSES.

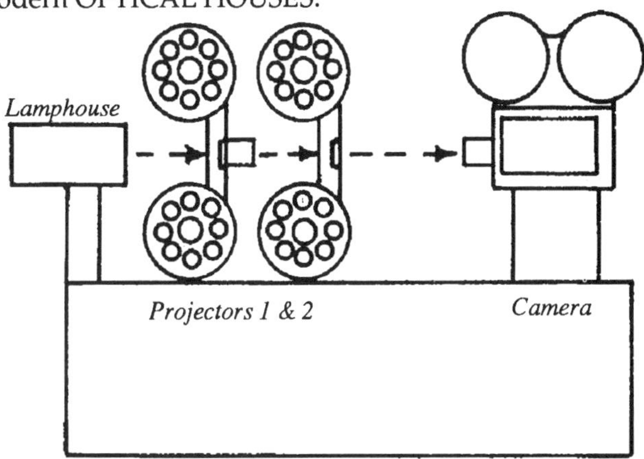

Simplified Optical Printer

OPTICAL PRINTING
The process of executing any of the many functions of an optical printer. For example: FREEZE FRAME PRINTING, SKIP PRINTING, BACK AND FORTH PRINTING, OPTICAL COMPOSITE PHOTOGRAPHY, OPTICAL ANIMATION, etc.

OPTICAL REDUCTION
The process of using an OPTICAL PRINTER to reduce a film image from a large FORMAT, such as VISTAVISION, to a smaller format such as standard 35 mm.

OPTICALS
A term loosely used to refer to any special effects shot which involves the combining of two or more images onto one piece of film.

OPTICAL SCANNER
A computer INPUT DEVICE which converts flat artwork or film transparencies into DIGITAL information. The scanner reads the color and brightness of light reflecting from or transmitting through the artwork or transparency and assigns numerical values in proportion to the readings.

OPTICAL ZOOM
The process of creating a ZOOM move into an filmed image using an OPTICAL PRINTER.

OPTICS
The glass components of a lens.

ORIGINAL
See CAMERA ORIGINAL and ORIGINAL NEGATIVE.

ORIGINAL NEGATIVE
The piece of NEGATIVE upon which a scene is first filmed.

OUT OF STEADY
A camera or projector movement which fails to perfectly register each frame of film in the FILM GATE is said to be "out of steady" or "unsteady." See STEADY and STEADINESS.

OUTPUT DEVICE
Any of several devices used to convert DIGITAL IMAGES into film images. For example: LASER PRINTER, SOLITAIRE.

OVERCRANKED
A scene which has been filmed at a frame rate in excess of normal sound speed of 24 frames per second has been "overcranked." See also UNDERCRANKED.

OVERDEVELOPMENT
See FORCED DEVELOPMENT.

OVEREXPOSE
To give a scene more exposure than normal such that it appears brighter on film than in real life. Opposite of UNDEREXPOSE.

OVERSIZE SET
A set which is built at a SCALE larger that life–size in order to make live actors appear to be smaller.

OVERSIZED SETS are used in this wagon chase scene from "Willow" to make the "Brownie" characters appear to be nine inches tall. Photo courtesy of Lucasfilm Ltd.

PADDLE
See BLUESCREEN PADDLE.

PAGE
The amount of computer memory required to store a complete image.

PAINTBOX™
A widely used video PAINT SYSTEM manufactured by Quantel.

PAINTED MATTE SHOT
See MATTE SHOT.

PAINTING
See MATTE PAINTING.

PAINT SYSTEM
Any COMPUTER GRAPHICS SOFTWARE SYSTEM which allows a user to draw or paint an image directly into memory using a DIGITIZING TABLE/TABLET and a DIGITIZING PEN. Paint systems can simulate any number of mediums common to the art world such as ink pens, airbrushes and paintbrushes.

PAL
An acronym for PHASE ALTERNATING LINE. The television broadcast standard for most of western Europe, delivering 625 lines of RESOLUTION compared to the U.S. standard of 525 lines.

PALETTE
In COMPUTER GRAPHICS or PAINT SYSTEM applications, the choice of colors available to the user. The number of colors available is directly related to the number of BITS which are dedicated to storing each PIXEL. The greater the number of bits, the greater the color selection. See COLOR DEPTH, 8 BIT COLOR, 16 BIT COLOR, 24 BIT COLOR.

PANAVISION™
A trademarked wide screen process using standard 35 mm film and ANAMORPHIC lenses to yield an ASPECT RATIO of 2.35:1. The name "Panavision" is commonly used to refer to all wide screen formats.

PARALLACTIC MOVEMENT
See PARALLAX.

PARALLAX
The natural phenomenon that occurs while moving a camera through space in which objects close to the camera pass through frame faster than objects in the distance. Multiplane camera systems seek to simulate this natural parallactic movement.

PARTICLE SYSTEM
A computer MODELING technique for creating a fluid object by tracking many small particles. Fire, water and explosions can be modeled in this way.

PASS

1) A single trip through a camera of a piece of film during which an exposure is made.
2) Each of several exposures made of a subject under differing lighting conditions. Examples of different types of passes would be: BEAUTY PASS, COLOR PASS, FOG PASS, LIGHT PASS, MATTE PASS, SMOKE PASS, etc.

PASS THROUGH EFFECT

The effect of one image "passing through" another achieved by DOUBLE EXPOSURE or selective MATTING.

PATCH

A curved, four sided shape used to more accurately model an object than can be accomplished with a POLYGON. (A patch looks like a "patch" on an elbow or knee.)

PEG BARS

Metal or plastic strips with special protruding pins called REGISTER PEGS that are used to position and hold animation drawings as they are being made or photographed.

PEG BOARD ANIMATION

Animation using artwork or drawings which are positioned onto paper or cels which have been pre–punched with REGISTER HOLES. These holes then position the artwork onto REGISTER PEGS fastened to the table of the ANIMATION STAND.

PENCIL TEST

A preliminary animation test in which rough pencil drawings or computer WIREFRAME MODELS are filmed or output to video in order to check movement prior to INKING or RENDERING. More often called a LINE TEST in COMPUTER GRAPHICS applications.

PERF

Abbreviation for PERFORATION.

PERF DAMAGE

Damage to a perforation caused by a maladjusted camera or projection system.

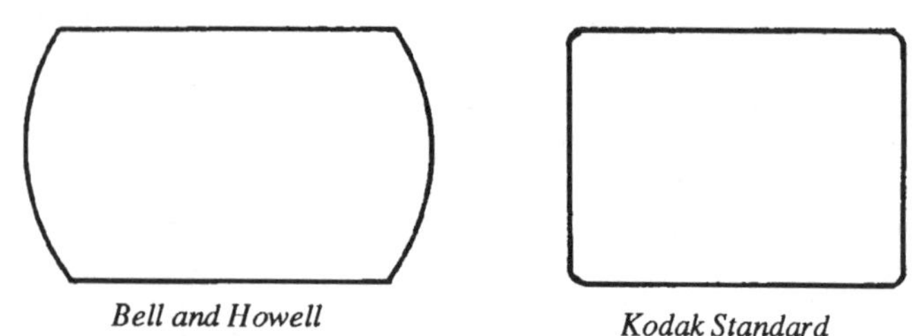

PERFORATIONS

PERFORATIONS
The sprocket holes which run along the sides of a piece of film. See KODAK STANDARD PERFORATION and BELL AND HOWELL PERFORATION.

PERFORATION PITCH
The distance between perforations as measured along one side of a piece of film.
(See FRAME illustration on page 55.)

PERFORATION TOLERANCE
The margin of error in the dimension of a perforation allowed by the manufacturer of a film stock. This margin of error allows the perforation at times to be larger or smaller than the typical REGISTRATION PIN. PERF PICKING seeks to identify a perforation which is exactly the size of the registration pin.

PERF PICKED
A film stock whose perforations have been measured for fit onto a REGISTRATION PIN is said to be "perf picked."

PERF PICKING
The process of measuring the perforations on a roll of film to determine which are the optimal size for perfect REGISTRATION. See PERFORATION TOLERANCE.

PERIPHERAL DEVICES
PRINTERS, MONITORS, INPUT SCANNERS, DIGITIZING TABLES/TABLETS, EXTERNAL DISC DRIVES are all peripheral devices, that is devices not immediately required for the computer to function.

PHOTOCHEMICAL PROCESS
Any photographic processes which rely on the photochemical reactions between light and film EMULSIONs, and development solutions.

PHOTO MATTE
A photograph which is placed into a scene to modify or extend the scene in much the same way as a MATTE PAINTING would accomplish.

PHOTO ROTO
A procedure in which each frame of a shot is printed onto a large piece of photostat paper which has been prepunched with holes for REGISTRATION onto a peg bar. These photos are then used as a reference guide when animating effects to be added to the scene.

PHOTOSHOP™
A sophisticated draw and paint SOFTWARE package for use on the Macintosh computer system.

PHYSICAL EFFECTS
See PRACTICAL EFFECTS.

PICKING PERFS
A maladjusted camera movement which causes minor perforation damage is "picking perfs."

PICTURE ELEMENT
A computer term which refers to a single microscopic point of information in a picture. More commonly abbreviated as PIXEL, a typical high resolution computer image is made up of hundreds of thousands of these points.

PICTURE FILE
A section of computer memory commonly called a FILE which contains all the data required to create an image.

PILOT PIN
The REGISTRATION pin in a camera or projector movement which is larger and closer fitting to the perforation than all others. The pilot pin positions the film in the gate while the other pins hold the film steady. Commonly referred to as the BIG PIN.
(See REGISTRATION PINS illustration on page 121.)

PINBLOCK
A small metal plate with two protruding REGISTRATION PINS onto which one or more pieces of film can be placed to aid in previewing an OPTICAL COMPOSITE.
(See illustration on page 110.)

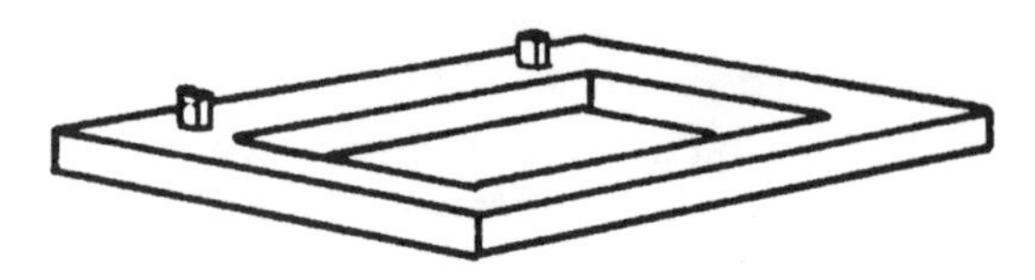

Pin Block

PINBLOCK DEVICE
An automated shuttle which positions and registers a piece of film under an animation camera for rephotography.

Pin Block Device *Photo courtesy of Lucasfilm Ltd.*

PINBLOCKED ELEMENT
An ELEMENT of a COMPOSITE which has been re–photographed under an animation stand with the use of a PINBLOCK DEVICE.

PIN REGISTERED
1) A camera or projector which employs REGISTRATION PINS is said to be "pin registered."
2) A print which has been made on an OPTICAL PRINTER which utilizes REGISTRATION PINS is said to be "pin registered."

PIN REGISTERED CAMERA
A camera which produces STEADY images through the use of REGISTRATION PINS.

PIN REGISTERED MOVEMENT
A camera or projector movement which utilizes REGISTRATION PINS for accurate positioning of the film in the FILM GATE.

PIN REGISTERED OPTICAL PRINTER
An OPTICAL PRINTER which has PIN REGISTERED MOVEMENTS in both projector and camera.

PIN REGISTRATION
The process of inserting REGISTRATION PINS into the perforations of each frame of film in order to precisely position and hold the film within a camera or projector movement. Perfect REGISTRATION of an image during exposure is critical to the success of most compositing processes. Without perfect registration, COMPOSITED images appear to "shake" or "vibrate" against each other.

PITCH
See PERFORATION PITCH

PIXAR™
A large FRAME BUFFER manufactured by Pixar Corporation which is used to manipulate DIGITAL IMAGES.

PIXEL
Abbreviation for PICTURE ELEMENT.

PIXEL MANIPULATION
The basis of IMAGE PROCESSING. Since pixel information is stored as a set of numbers, various arithmetic and logical operations can be applied to this data for any number of results, including IMAGE SHARPENING, IMAGE MORPHING, etc.

PIXILATION
A form of STOP MOTION ANIMATION which often uses humans as subject and achieves rapid and intentionally jerky movements which are comical in nature.

PLATE
A live action scene usually involving principal actors shot in coordination with the first or second units of a production. For example, a BLUESCREEN shot involving actors is called a "BLUESCREEN PLATE;" a live action scene to be used as a BACKGROUND in a COMPOSITE shot is called a "BACKGROUND PLATE." See also BACKGROUND PLATE.

PLOTTING
The process of duplicating a camera move by projecting a scene filmed with a moving camera onto a flat surface and

tracking on paper the relative position in frame of a fixed object in the scene. The various camera positions are programmed into a MOTION CONTROL system for playback during the shooting of additional MATCHED MOVE ELEMENTS.

POLARIZED LIGHT
Light composed of rays which vibrate along one plane only, as opposed to normal light whose rays vibrate randomly. Light can become polarized by reflecting off glass or water surfaces, by refracting through a clear sky, or by passing through a polarizing filter. During outdoor photography such polarized light is usually filtered out due to its tendency to produce glare. Polarized light, in combination with the proper use of POLARIZING FILTERS on the camera lens, is used during the photography of MATTE PAINTINGS and ANIMATION artwork to eliminate brushstrokes and dust. See POLARIZING FILTER.

POLARIZING FILTER
A filter which has the capacity to absorb all light rays vibrating along a particular plane. This type of filter is useful in eliminating unwanted glare from a windshield or wet surface. When used in combination with a polarized light source, a polarizing filter can eliminate specular highlights caused by dust or brush strokes on an animated drawing or MATTE PAINTING.

POLARIZING SCREEN
See POLARIZING FILTER.

POLA SCREEN
See POLARIZING FILTER.

POLYGON
A geometric figure or shape created with the help of a computer. Polygons are a complex series of interconnecting planar surfaces which approximate the shape of a three dimensional subject. A geodesic dome could be considered a polygon of a sphere.

POLYGONAL MODELING
The process of approximating the shape of a three dimensional subject by creating a surface comprised of a complex

series of small interconnecting planar surfaces. A geodesic dome could be considered a polygon of a sphere.

POSITIVE
A piece of film in which the colors and light values correspond to the original subject (as opposed to a negative image.) A positive is generated by making a print from a negative.

POSITIVE IMAGE
1) An image in which the colors and light values correspond to those of the original scene.
2) The image on a piece of positive film.

POSITIVE PERFORATION
See KODAK STANDARD PERFORATION.

POSITIVE PITCH
The distance between perforations measured along one side of a piece of positive film, which is slightly greater than that of a piece of negative film.
(See FRAME illustrationon page 55.)

POST PRODUCTION
The period of time following the completion of PRINCIPAL PHOTOGRAPHY during which editing, sound effects editing, music scoring, VISUAL EFFECTS, and any other unfinished work is completed.

POWERS OF TEN SHOT
A shot which starts close on a subject and proceeds to widen exponentially as though the camera is being lifted into space. (Or the reverse action.) These type of shots are often included at the beginning or end of a film or commercial for dramatic impact.

PRACTICAL
A term used to distinguish between working and non–working set pieces or decorations. Practical lights, for example, are lights which both contribute to the lighting of a scene and serve a decorative purpose. Set doors which function or a sink with running water would also be considered practical.

PRACTICAL EFFECTS
Special effects which are performed at the time of principal photography without the use of photographic tricks. For

example: wind effects, bullet hits, and explosions. See also MECHANICAL EFFECTS.

PRE COMP
Abbreviation for PRELIMINARY COMPOSITE.

PRE COMPOSITE
Abbreviation for PRELIMINARY COMPOSITE.

PREFLASHING
A FLASH exposed onto a negative prior to a scene being filmed in order to control the CONTRAST of that scene.

PREFOGGING
See PREFLASHING.

PRELIMINARY COMPOSITE
A COMPOSITE using the primary ELEMENTS of a shot, such as the BACKGROUND and principal FOREGROUND, which is made as an action and position reference for the creation of additional elements. Commonly referred to as a PRE COMP.

PRE–PRODUCTION
The period of time prior to the beginning of PRINCIPAL PHOTOGRAPHY during which a motion picture production is prepared.

PRIMARY COLORS
1) ADDITIVE PRIMARY COLORS. In photography, the colors red, green and blue of which all other colors are combinations. When additive primary colors are mixed in equal measures, white light is the result.
2) SUBTRACTIVE PRIMARY COLORS. The colors cyan, magenta and yellow, each of which is obtained by subtracting one of the ADDITIVE PRIMARY COLORS from white light. The absence of red makes cyan; the absence of green makes magenta; the absence of blue makes yellow. See COLOR TRIANGLE.

PRIMER CORD
A powerfully explosive fuse–like material commonly used in pyrotechnics to blow things up without generating smoke or flames.

PRINCIPAL PHOTOGRAPHY
The portion of a movie filmed by the first and second units consisting of all the principal scenes involving actors, stunts and other major logistical considerations.

PRINT
A POSITIVE image made from a NEGATIVE.

PRINTBACK
A duplicate of an image made onto negative film stock. A printback of a NEGATIVE image will be a POSITIVE image, and vice verse.

PRINTER
Any device which is used to duplicate a film image.

PRINTING STOCK
See PRINT STOCK.

PRINT STOCK
Any of the various film stocks used to make a positive image from a negative.

PRINT THROUGH
When a BACKGROUND ELEMENT is visible through a foreground element, the BACKGROUND is said to "print through" the foreground image. Print through is usually caused by MATTES which are not of sufficient density to HOLD OUT the BACKGROUND image.

PRISM
See PRISM BEAM SPLITTER.

PRISM BEAM SPLITTER
A special piece of glass used to divide incoming light rays into two or more identical beams of light. Prisms are often used behind the lens of a camera to divide an image and send one portion to the film plane while diverting a second portion to the viewfinder. Prisms are also commonly used to split a single LASER source into multiple sources.

PROCESS CAMERA
A camera with critically accurate REGISTRATION which is used in the production of VISUAL EFFECTS.

PROCESS PHOTOGRAPHY
A common term referring to FRONT or REAR PROJECTION.

PROCESS PLATE
A BACKGROUND ELEMENT to be used in either FRONT or REAR PROJECTION.

PROCESS PROJECTION
A common term referring to FRONT or REAR PROJECTION.

PROCESS PROJECTOR
A motion picture or still projector used in FRONT or REAR PROJECTION processes.

PROCESS SCREEN
A FRONT or REAR PROJECTION screen.

PROCESS SHOT
Any shot which is to be COMPOSITED with either FRONT or REAR PROJECTION.

PROCESS UNIT
A film production unit which is responsible for either FRONT or REAR PROJECTION photography.

PRODUCTION
The name given to the period of time during which the PRINCIPAL PHOTOGRAPHY of a motion picture is accomplished. Also generally refers to the process of making a motion picture.

PROJECTION, BACK
See REAR PROJECTION.

PROJECTION, FRONT
See FRONT PROJECTION.

PROJECTION, PROCESS
See PROCESS PROJECTION.

PROJECTION, REAR
See REAR PROJECTION.

PROJECTOR MOVEMENT
The mechanical apparatus in a projector which intermittently advances the film to the next frame and holds it in position while the shutter is open. See also CAMERA MOVEMENT.

PROSTHETIC MAKEUP APPLIANCE
A sheet of latex rubber which has been sculpted and formed to fit the face of an actor in order to change his features. Various creatures or wounds can be made using prosthetic appliances.

PROSTHETICS
See PROSTHETIC MAKEUP APPLIANCES.

PROTECTION NEGATIVE
A copy of the ORIGINAL NEGATIVE which is made as insurance against damage to the original.

PROTECTION PLATE
An additional take of an acceptable BACKGROUND plate which is shot as protection against possible future damage to the preferred take.

PUCK
Nickname for CROSSHAIR DIGITIZER originating from the fact that early versions looked a lot like a hockey puck.

PULL
To underdevelop a roll of film to compensate for overexposure of the negative during filming. See UNDERDEVELOPMENT.

PULL A MATTE
The process of making a DIFFERENCE MATTE with an OPTICAL PRINTER.

PULLDOWN CLAW
The portion of a camera movement which serves to advance the film through the FILM GATE. See CAMERA MOVEMENT.

PULLDOWN MENU
A secondary menu which normally is hidden behind the MENU BAR at the top of a COMPUTER SCREEN. A pulldown menu is revealed by using a MOUSE to position the CURSOR over a select portion of the menu bar and "pulling" the cursor down to reveal the new menu.

PUPPET ANIMATION
See STOP MOTION ANIMATION.

PUSH
To overdevelop a roll of film to compensate for underexposure. See FORCED DEVELOPMENT.

PYLON
A combination model–mount and model–mover device which is covered with neon–lit BLUESCREEN material for use in BLUESCREEN model photography.

PYRO/PYROTECHNICS
The use of smoke, fire or explosives to achieve an effect.

RAR
An acronym for RAPID ACCESS RECOVERY, a type of black and white film stock used to shoot film tests of camera setups before shooting color film. The advantage of RAR is that it can be quickly processed with minimal equipment.

RASTER
The set of horizontal lines scanned by an electron beam in a CRT as an image is displayed.

RASTER DISPLAY
A device which organizes an image into multiple rows of PIXELS for DISPLAY, such as a common television screen. An analogous display would be the way a typewriter creates text on a piece of paper one line at a time.

RASTER GRAPHICS
See COMPUTER GRAPHICS.

RAWSTOCK
A fresh piece of film which has received no exposure to light.

RAY TRACING
A realistic RENDERING technique used in COMPUTER GRAPHICS to accurately create the surfaces of reflective or refractive subjects.

REAL TIME
The amount of time in which an event would naturally occur, as opposed to SLOW MOTION, TIME LAPSE, or STOP MOTION.

REAL TIME MOTION CONTROL
A MOTION CONTROL system which can record and play-back camera moves at REAL TIME. See FIELD RECORDER and VISTAGLIDE.

REAR LIT ANIMATION
See BOTTOM LIT ANIMATION.

REAR LIT BLUESCREEN
See TRANSMISSION BLUESCREEN.

REAR PROJECTION
A compositing process which involves placing a subject in front of a large translucent screen onto which a BACKGROUND image is projected from behind. See also FRONT PROJECTION.
(See illustration below.)

REAR PROJECTION PHOTOGRAPHY
See REAR PROJECTION.

REAR PROJECTION SCREEN
A translucent screen onto which an image is projected during rear projection photography.

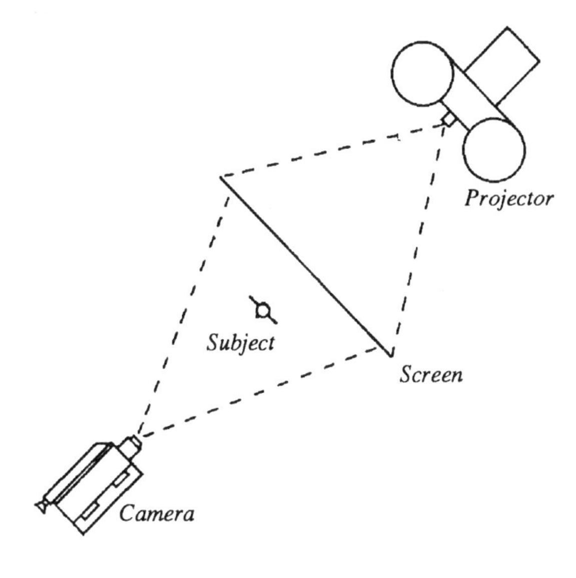

REAR PROJECTION

RECIPROCITY FAILURE
The failure of the law which states *exposure = intensity x duration* (reciprocity), to hold up during long exposure times.

RED RECORD
See COLOR SEPARATIONS.

REDUCTION
The use of an OPTICAL PRINTER to convert a film image from a large format such as Vistavision to a smaller format such as standard 35 mm.

REDUCTION ONLY
See REDUCTION ONLY COMPOSITE.

REDUCTION ONLY COMPOSITE
The OPTICAL REDUCTION of a shot which was filmed in large format for use as a special effects BACKGROUND, but which subsequently includes no effect as the result of a change of plan.

REDUCTION PRINT
A 35 mm print made from a larger negative such as Vistavision. Reduction prints are used to edit BACKGROUND PLATES into a scene to determine exactly which part of the plate is to be used.

REDUCTION ROLLS
Rolls of standard 35 mm GAUGE POSITIVE (print) which have been reduced from a larger format negative for editing into the movie.

REFERENCE CLIPS
Short pieces of film which have been clipped from the body of a shot for lighting and color reference.

REFLECTION MAPPING
A technique used in COMPUTER GRAPHICS in which the environment surrounding a subject is placed as reflections onto the surfaces of the subject. See IMAGE MAPPING.

REFLECTIVE LIGHT METER
Also called a SPOT METER, a light measuring instrument used to determine the amount of light reflecting off the surface of a subject. Such meters measure the amount of light reflecting off a certain "spot" of the subject as opposed to an INCIDENT METER which measures all the light falling on the subject.

REGISTERED PRINT
A print which has been made on a PIN REGISTERED OPTICAL PRINTER. Registered prints are essential whenever steadiness of the image is required such as for ROTOSCOPING or PLOTTING procedures.

REGISTER HOLES
Holes which are punched into animation artwork allowing the accurate positioning of each piece of art onto REGISTER PEGS.

REGISTER PEGS
Pins or dowels which are fastened to an animator's easel, light table or an animation stand which allow each piece of animated art to be accurately positioned relative to all others.

Register Pegs

REGISTRATION
The process of accurately aligning the position of a series of images or frames.

REGISTRATION HOLES
See REGISTER HOLES.

REGISTRATION PEGS
See REGISTER PEGS.

REGISTRATION PINS
The metal pins in the movement of a camera or projector which position and hold the film in preparation for exposure. See PILOT PIN and PIN REGISTRATION.

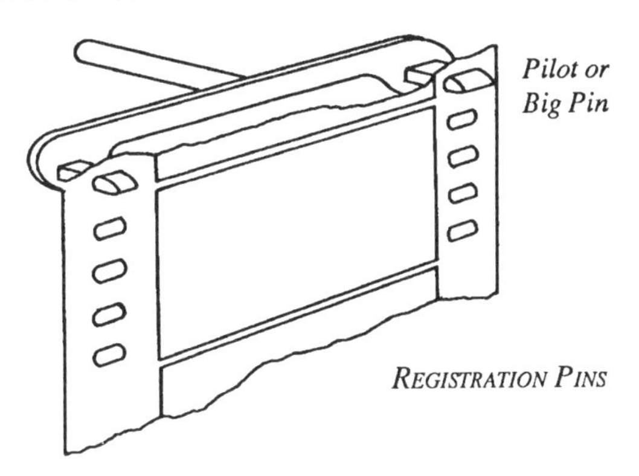

Registration Pins

RELAY LENS
A lens in an OPTICAL PRINTER which evenly focuses light from a condenser lens onto the film plane.

RELEASE PRINT
A print of a finished film complete with sound track and visuals.

REMOVABLE HARD DISC
A cartridge style HARD DISC which can be removed from the disc drive unit.

RENDERING
A small full color painting which illustrates what an effects shot will ultimately look like. Also, the process of RENDERING AN IMAGE in COMPUTER GRAPHICS.

RENDERING AN IMAGE
A COMPUTER GRAPHICS process of creating the final detail and color of a computer generated image.

RENDERMAN™
A trademarked SOFTWARE system developed by Pixar Corporation to create high quality three dimensional computer generated images.

REPEATABLE
The ability of a computerized machine or mechanism to exactly repeat a move. Repeatability is a critical requirement of MOTION CONTROL SYSTEMS.

REPO/REPOSITION
To adjust the position of an ELEMENT within the frame.

RESIZING
The process in COMPUTER GRAPHICS of enlarging or reducing an image by increasing or decreasing the number of PIXELS used to define the image. Also called SCALING.

RESOLUTION
The degree of detail in an image. In COMPUTER GRAPHICS, resolution refers to the number of horizontal lines of PIXELS which make up an image. In film, resolution is related to the size of the individual particles of grain.

RESOLVING POWER
The measurable ability of a lens to distinguish minute detail in a scene.

RETICLE
The image scribed in the ground glass of a viewing system which delineates the frame boundaries of the image being filmed.

REVEAL MATTE
An animated MATTE which is used to progressively uncover an image. For example, a line animating across a scene might be executed with a mask which progressively reveals more and more of one continuous line. Also called a WIPE MATTE.

REVERSE ACTION (PRINTING)
The process of printing a scene in reverse such that the first frame becomes the last and all motion reverses direction.

REVERSE BLUESCREEN PROCESS
A process developed by Apogee, Inc., which uses phosphorescent paint to "reverse" a normal bluescreen image. A subject is coated with clear lacquer which contains phosphors which glow when illuminated with ultra–violet light. The resultant image is a "glowing"' subject against a black BACKGROUND which can be used as a MATTE.

REVERSE MOTION
See REVERSE ACTION.

REVERSE PRINTING
See REVERSE ACTION.

RGB
Refers to red, green and blue, the ADDITIVE PRIMARY COLORS of light.

RIPPLE EFFECT
The effect of looking through heat waves, which is often used to suggest a dream sequence. Ripple effects are created by shooting through a piece of moving RIPPLE GLASS.

RIPPLE GLASS
A sheet of textured or visually flawed glass or plastic used to distort an image. Textured shower door glass is a favorite example of ripple glass.

RITTER™
A large gasoline–engine propelled fan used to create large scale wind effects.

ROTOSCOPE

a. Original BLUESCREEN scene with stunt pad to be removed. (The blurred image is the result of natural motion blur during photography.)

b. ROTO ARTIST Tom Bertino hard at work tracing the outline of the character. Tom must decide exactly where to define the edges of the blurred character for each frame. Inconsistent positioning of this edge from frame to frame will create a CHEWING problem.

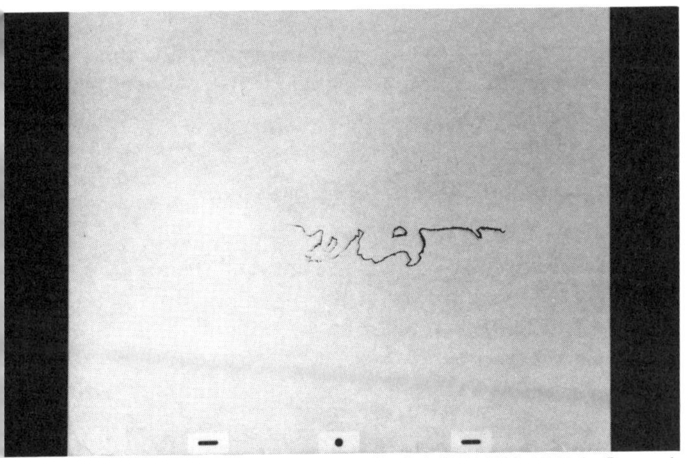

c. The rotoscoped drawing before inking.

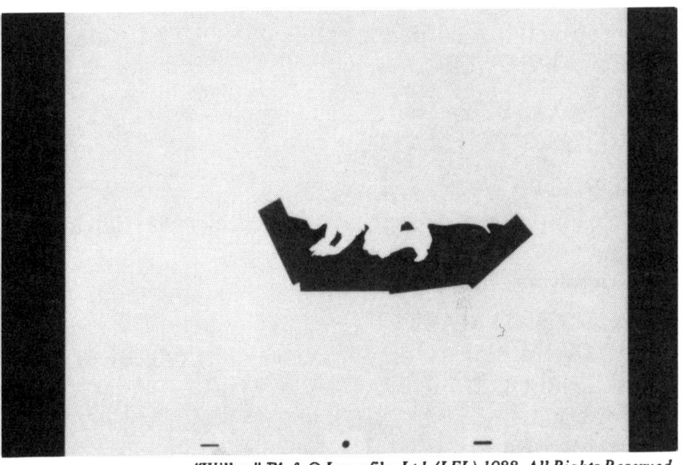

d. The finished rotoscoped matte which is used in combination with other mattes to completely extract the character from the bluescreen background.

ALL PHOTOS COURTESY OF LUCASFILM LTD.

ROBOTICS
The creation of automated creatures or characters which function on the set via remote control. Also called ANIMATRONIC.

ROCK AND ROLL
See BACK AND FORTH PRINTING.

ROD ARTICULATE MATTE
A hand drawn MATTE used to eliminate from a COMPOSITE the model support rods unavoidably filmed as part of a BLUESCREEN ELEMENT.
(See illustration on page 90.)

ROD PUPPET
A puppet which is articulated continuously during slow motion photography through the use of rods and wires.
(See color photo on page 94.)

ROTO ARTIST
A person who rotoscopes. See ROTOSCOPE and ROTOSCOPE STAND.

ROTO MATTE
See ROTOSCOPED MATTE.

ROTOSCOPE
To trace onto paper an image which is projected from a piece of film.
(See illustration on pages 124-125.)

ROTOSCOPED MATTE
A MATTE which is hand drawn under a ROTOSCOPE STAND, including BLUE SPILL MATTES, ARTICULATE MATTES, ROD ARTICULATE MATTES and GARBAGE MATTES.
(See illustration on pages 124-125.)

ROTOSCOPE STAND
An ANIMATION STAND dedicated to the rotoscoping process. It consists of a camera into which processed film is loaded and a light source which shines from behind the film plane, through the lens, onto a table outfitted with register pegs. The filmed images are traced onto paper accurately positioned onto these register pegs. Once the rotoscoped tracings are completed, the light source is removed, fresh film is loaded into the camera and the rotoscoped drawings can be rephotographed in perfect REGISTRATION with the original film image. Rotoscope

stands are used to create ROD ARTICULATE MATTES, BLUE SPILL MATTES, and GARBAGE MATTES, etc.

ROTO STAND
See ROTOSCOPE STAND.

ROUGH COMP
See ROUGH COMPOSITE.

ROUGH COMPOSITE
A quick and dirty color COMPOSITE used to verify that the various ELEMENTS of a shot are working in conjunction with each other. The rough comp is cut into the movie for approval by the director before further work is continued. Also called 5272, 5272 COMP, 5272 COMPOSITE or ROUGH COMP.

RP
Abbreviation for REAR PROJECTION.

RUBBER STAMP
A technique in COMPUTER GRAPHICS of copying a certain portion of an image over and over again, much as a rubber stamp can be used to place multiple images of the same subject onto a piece of paper.

RUSHES
See DAILIES.

S

SAFE ACTION AREA
The area within a 35 mm film frame which is not subject to possible deletion during television broadcast. All critical action must be within this area, which encompasses approximately 90 percent of the screen.

SAFE TITLE AREA
The area within a 35 mm film frame in which all titles must appear to eliminate possible deletion during television broadcast. Safe title area includes roughly the center 80 percent of the screen.

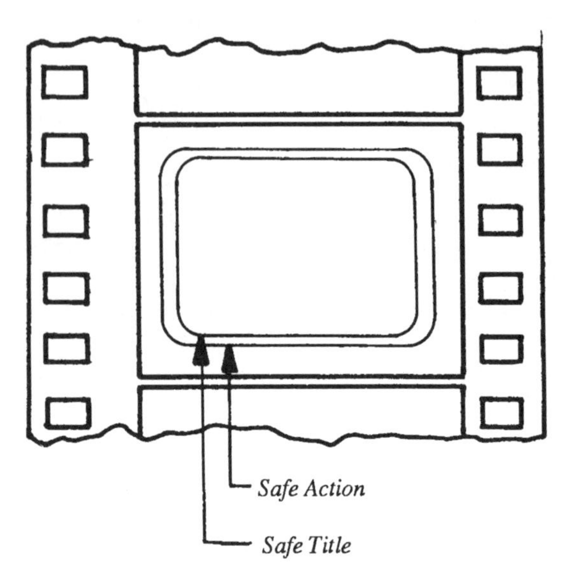

SAMPLE
A measurement at any particular point in time. For example, a MOTION CONTROL computer samples the speed of motors operated from a JOYSTICK many times per second in order to replicate the action.

SAMPLE RATE
The frequency with which a computer takes a data sample. This can relate to the number of samples per second taken of a motor's movement, or to the proximity of KEY POINTS of a graphic image entered into the computer from a DIGITIZING TABLE/TABLET.

SATURATION
The degree of purity of a color. See also DESATURATION.

SCALE
The size of a model expressed as a fractional number of the actual size of the subject. For example a model which is one-fourth the size of the original is "one quarter scale."

SCALING
See RESIZING.

SCAN IN
The use of an INPUT SCANNER to convert film images into DIGITAL images. See DIGITIZE.

SCAN LINE
One horizontal pass of an electron beam or LASER beam across an image during DISPLAY on a MONITOR or during INPUT or OUTPUT SCANNING.

SCAN OUT
The use of an OUTPUT DEVICE to convert DIGITAL images into film images.

SCENE
A shot or sequence of shots in a motion picture.

SCOTCHLIGHT
See SCOTCHLITE.

SCOTCHLITE™
See FRONT PROJECTION SCREEN.

SCOTCHLITE SCREEN
See FRONT PROJECTION SCREEN.

SECOND GENERATION
See GENERATION.

SECOND GENERATION DUPE
A copy made from a CAMERA ORIGINAL. That is, a DUPLICATE NEGATIVE which is made from a FIRST GENERATION NEGATIVE.

SELSYN MOTOR
See STEPPER MOTOR.

SEMI–TRANSPARENT MIRROR
See FIFTY–FIFTY MIRROR.

SENSITOMETER
An instrument used to place a controlled EXPOSURE WEDGE onto a piece of film for the purpose of evaluating a film EMULSION or development process.

SENSITOMETRIC STRIP
The piece of film onto which an EXPOSURE WEDGE is placed by a SENSITOMETER.

SENSITOMETRY
The study of the effects of light on film EMULSIONs.

SEPARATION MASTERS
Three separate POSITIVE black and white films onto which the red, green and blue components of a color image are recorded. See COLOR SEPARATIONS.

SEPARATION POSITIVES
See SEPARATION MASTERS.

SEPS
Abbreviation for COLOR SEPARATIONS.

SERVO MOTOR
A self–regulating motor whose speed is controlled by the use of crystal oscillators. Also known as a CRYSTAL MOTOR.

70 mm FORMAT
Wide screen film gauge which uses a 65 mm negative. SEE 65 mm.

SFX
Special effects. Also abbreviated FX.

SHADING
The process of RENDERING a computer generated object with shadows and highlights based on a directional source of light.

SHARPENING FILTER
A COMPUTER GRAPHICS procedure of enhancing the detail in an image to achieve the impression of greater SHARPNESS. Also called a HIGH–PASS FILTER

SHOT ON ONES/TWOS
See ON ONES/TWOS.

SHOWSCAN™
A trademarked special use large screen format which uses 70 mm film shot and projected at 60 frames per second. Douglas Trumbull pioneered the process to eliminate the perception of grain, flicker and image strobing common in standard format films. The resulting image has a "real" almost three–dimensional look.

SHUTTER ANGLE
The angular measure of the opening of a rotating shutter, the greater the shutter angle, the longer the exposure time given to a piece of negative.

SHUTTER SPEED
The length of time a shutter is opened to allow light to expose a frame of film. Shutter speeds are measured in seconds or fractions thereof.

SHUTTLE
A type of camera or projector movement. See CAMERA MOVEMENT.

SINGLE FRAME CAMERA
A camera which exposes one frame of film at a time.

SINGLE FRAME EXPOSURE
The exposure of only one frame of film at a time.

SINGLE FRAME MOTOR
A camera motor designed to expose one frame of film at a time.

SIXTEEN BIT COLOR
Refers to the number of color possibilities for COMPUTER GENERATED IMAGERY when each PIXEL is stored as 16 bits of information, or roughly 65,000 colors. See EIGHT BIT COLOR and TWENTY–FOUR BIT COLOR and THIRTY–TWO BIT COLOR.

65 mm FILM
A standard film GAUGE for camera negative which is then printed onto 70 mm print stock to yield the popular wide screen format. The negative is 65 mm wide and has several times the image area of the standard 35 mm frame. Though few films are photographed in 65 mm due to the extra cost of the larger film stock, the gauge is still commonly used in special effects processes due to the high resolution of the large negative.

SKIP FRAME PRINTING
See SKIP PRINTING.

SKIP FRAMING
See SKIP PRINTING.

SKIP OUT
The elimination of one or more frames while printing a scene in order to correct for accidental DOUBLE FRAMES or to speed up a specific bit of action.

SKIP PRINTING
The process of printing every other frame, or every third frame, or every fourth frame, etc., in order to speed up the action of a shot.

SLAVE MOTOR
A motor which mimics the motion of a MASTER MOTOR or an OPTICAL ENCODER. This dual motor concept is the basis for many remote control camera systems such as the popular Hot Head.

SLIP THE SYNC
To change the relative timing of two or more separate ELEMENTS within a shot by "slipping" their relative starting points. Such an adjustment could be made for a multitude of reasons, primary of which is to increase the dramatic impact of the interaction of the various shot ELEMENTS.

SLIT SCAN
An effects animation process which produces streaked images by using long exposure times coupled with camera and artwork moves while filming through a small slit in a foreground barrier. This complex combination of moves produces a more three dimensional looking image than normal streak photography.

Slit Scan

SLOW MOTION PHOTOGRAPHY
The technique of filming a scene at higher that normal frame rates so that the action will appear to be slowed down when projected at 24 frames per second.

SODIUM PROCESS
See SODIUM VAPOR TRAVELING MATTE PROCESS.

SODIUM VAPOR TRAVELING MATTE PROCESS
A TRAVELING MATTE process used by Walt Disney Studios which utilizes a yellow sodium vapor light source as the background rather than a BLUESCREEN. The image of the subject against the yellow field is filmed with a dual negative camera onto two separate negatives, one black and white which forms a MATTE, and the other color. This process is especially useful when the subject being filmed is blue, a color the normal BLUESCREEN PROCESS cannot accommodate.

SOFT COPY
Temporary DISPLAY or storage of images or information such as those on a video MONITOR, computer memory, or magnetic tape. See also HARD–COPY.

SOFT–EDGED MATTE
A MATTE which has a softly graduated edge as opposed to a sharp and well defined edge.

SOFTWARE
The programs and data which run a computer.

SOLARIZATION
A partial reversal of tonal gradation which occurs in an image which has been excessively overexposed. Sometimes this effect is intentionally utilized to alter the appearance of an image such as for use as the point of view of a creature or machine.

SOLITAIRE
A film OUTPUT DEVICE used to convert DIGITAL images into film images.

SONIC CLEANER
Abbreviation for ULTRASONIC CLEANER.

SOUND SPEED
The normal motion picture frame rate of 24 frames per second.

SOUTH
A term borrowed from the compass referring to the bottom portion of an image or frame.

SPECIAL EFFECTS
A term generally referring to all PRACTICAL, mechanical and visual effects. See SPECIAL VISUAL EFFECTS, PHYSICAL EFFECTS and MECHANICAL EFFECTS.

SPECIAL VISUAL EFFECTS
Special effects which are primarily accomplished after the conclusion of PRINCIPAL PHOTOGRAPHY, including OPTICALS, MATTE PAINTINGS, STOP and GO–MOTION PHOTOGRAPHY, ANIMATION EFFECTS, and MINIATURE PHOTOGRAPHY. In common usage the terms "Special Effects" and "Special Visual Effects" are interchanged.

SPHERICAL LENS
A lens which photographs a scene without the horizontal compression of an ANAMORPHIC LENS, yielding the ASPECT RATIOS of 1.33:1, 1.66:1 or 1.85:1.

SPILL LIGHT
1) Any unwanted light falling on a subject to be filmed.
2) In BLUESCREEN photography, spill light specifically refers to any unwanted light which strikes the surface of the bluescreen. Spill light on a bluescreen must be avoided in order to preserve the deep blue color of the screen.

SPILL MATTE
See BLUE SPILL MATTE.

SPLINES
A method in COMPUTER GRAPHICS of simulating smooth curves by connecting a large number of very short straight lines.

SPLIT MATTE
A hand drawn MATTE which divides the frame into two or more sections such that separate images may be placed in each section.

SPLIT SCREEN
The process of dividing a film frame into segments which each then contains a separate image. Split screens may be obvious, as in MULTI–IMAGE EFFECTS, or an invisible joining of two similar images. They can be filmed IN–CAM-

ERA or in POST PRODUCTION such as with the use of an OPTICAL PRINTER.

SPLIT SCREEN EFFECT
Any visual effect which divides the FRAME into distinct sections, each containing a separate image.

SPOT METER
A light measuring device used to determine the amount of light reflecting off the surface of a subject. Such meters measure the amount of light reflecting off a certain "spot" of the subject as opposed to an INCIDENT METER which measures all the light falling on the subject.

SQUASH
To FORESHORTEN an object. A subject is often "squashed" during animation to imply a deceleration within a scene. See also STRETCH.

SQUEEZE RATIO
The numerical ratio by which an ANAMORPHIC lens compresses the horizontal AXIS of an image to be photographed. A common squeeze ratio for anamorphic film formats is 2:1.

SQUIB
A small explosive device used in special effects to simulate bullet hits or mini explosions.

STAIRCASING
See ALIASING.

STAIRSTEPPING
See ALIASING.

STARFIELD
An expanse of stars as if seen in outer space.

STAR FILTER
A special effects filter which scatters specular sources of light into radially diverging beams of light.

STAR SCREEN
See STAR FILTER.

STEADINESS
Refers to the critical need in COMPOSITE photography for each frame of a filmed image to appear in precisely the same position relative to the perforations. An unsteady image, when composited, would appear to float or jiggle against the

BACKGROUND of a scene. Steadiness is an elusive condition of camera and OPTICAL PRINTER movements which requires a great deal of maintenance. Image steadiness is also critically related to the accurate size and condition of the perforations of a piece of film.

STEADY

1) A camera or projector movement is said to be "steady" if it registers each frame of film in precisely the same position relative to the APERTURE.
2) A filmed image is said to be steady if each image occupies precisely the same position relative to the perforations.

STEADY TEST

1) A test performed on a camera or projector movement to determine if it is STEADY. This can be accomplished by superimposing a suitable target (for instance a FIELD CHART) over a similar target filmed by a camera with known steadiness. If no proven steady camera is available, the next best thing is to superimpose two PASSes through the same camera of the target onto one piece of film. In either case, if the filmed images of the targets are locked together, the movement is said to be "steady."
2) A test performed on a negative or INTERMEDIATE ELEMENT to determine whether or not the image on film is steady. This involves making a duplicate of the image onto negative film stock which then receives a second exposure to a steady target.

STEPPER MOTOR

A motor whose revolutions are divided into numerous addressable segments. The fact that these motors can be directed to make any number of complete or fractional rotations makes MOTION CONTROL possible.

STEP PRINT

The optical technique of superimposing a grouping of consecutive frames of a moving image onto each frame of a new shot. The procedure yields a multiple exposure of for example, frames one through five of the old image onto frame one of the new image, frames two through six of the old image onto frame two of the new image, frames three through seven of the old image onto frame three of the new image, etc. This produces the effect of an image gently trailing itself as it moves through frame.

STEP PRINTER
See INTERMITTENT PRINTER.

STEREOSCOPIC PHOTOGRAPHY
A motion picture photographic technique which creates the illusion of three–dimensional images on a flat screen giving the audience the sensation of spacial relationship between various planes. Commonly referred to as 3–D.

STEWART T–MATTE™
A trademarked name for a translucent and flexible primary blue plastic material manufactured for the sole purpose of making BLUESCREENs. Refers to STEWART TRAVELING MATTE.

STEWART TRAVELING MATTE
See STEWART T–MATTE.

STILL STORE
See FRAME STORE.

STOP FRAME ANIMATION
See STOP MOTION ANIMATION.

STOP FRAME PHOTOGRAPHY
See STOP MOTION PHOTOGRAPHY.

STOP MOTION ANIMATION
The technique of photographing miniature puppets one frame at a time while manually adjusting their poses. The procedure involves moving the body and appendages of the puppet in small increments, shooting a frame of film, moving the puppet again, shooting another frame, etc.
(See photo on page 138.)

STOP MOTION ANIMATOR
The person who articulates a puppet during STOP MOTION ANIMATION.

STOP MOTION PHOTOGRAPHY
The process of filming a continuous action one frame at a time.

STORYBOARD
One or more drawings which illustrate the major elements, action, composition, camera moves and intent of a shot. They aid in communicating an idea to a group of people and are essential in all effects work.

STOP MOTION ANIMATOR Phil Tippett adjusts position of Snow Walker for a scene from "The Empire Strikes Back." Metal pointing device (SURFACE GAUGE) is used to verify how far the puppet is moved. Photo courtesy of Lucasfilm Ltd.

STREAK PASS
A pass auxiliary to the BEAUTY PASS in which the subject is caused to streak through the frame with the use of STREAK PHOTOGRAPHY.

STREAK PHOTOGRAPHY
A photographic technique in which camera moves combined with long exposure times produce streaked images, for example the HYPERSPACE streaking stars effect from "Star Wars."

STRETCH
To elongate an object. A subject is often "stretched" during animation to imply an acceleration within a scene. See also SQUASH.

STROBING
The apparent jerkiness in the movement of a subject caused by a lack of MOTION BLUR in STOP MOTION PHOTOGRAPHY. Also the staccato movement across frame of images filmed while panning the camera too fast.

STYLUS
See DIGITIZING PEN.

SUBTRACTIVE COLORS
See SUBTRACTIVE PRIMARY COLORS.

SUBTRACTIVE PRIMARY COLORS
In photography, the colors cyan, magenta and yellow, each of which is obtained by the absence of one of the ADDITIVE PRIMARY COLORS from white light. The absence of red makes cyan; the absence of green makes magenta; the absence of blue makes yellow. When mixed in equal proportion the three subtractive primary colors of light yield black. See COLOR TRIANGLE.
(See illustration on page 93.)

SUPER
Abbreviation for SUPERIMPOSE or SUPERIMPOSITION.

SUPER EAGLE DRIVE™
A computer disc drive which holds 660 megabytes, or 660 million bytes of data.

SUPERIMPOSE
The exposure of two or more images onto the same piece of film without the benefit of MATTING techniques. SUPERIMPOSITION allows each image to be seen through, or BLEED THROUGH the other.

SUPERIMPOSITION
The result of two images being photographed or printed over each other.

SUPER 35
A 35 mm film format in which maximum image area of the negative is used. Super 35 differs from standard 35 mm in that the image is centered on the negative with no room to the left of frame for the soundtrack. Super 35 offers the primary advantage ofshooting with spherical lenses while retaining the option to extract 1.33, 1.66, 1.85, ANAMORPHIC, or 70 mm wide screen format release prints at a later date. See also FORMAT and ASPECT RATIO.
See FORMAT illustrations on page 52-53.)

SURFACE GAUGE
A device used in STOP MOTION ANIMATION to aid in the determination of how far a puppet has been moved by the animator. A metal pointer rising from a heavy metal base is

positioned adjacent to the portion of the puppet to be moved, such that once it is moved a small gap exists between puppet and gauge. In this way incremental movements can be accurately made from one frame to the next.
(See STOP MOTION ANIMATION illustration on page 138.)

SURFACE RENDERING
The COMPUTER GRAPHICS technique of creating only the three dimensional external surfaces of an object with no description of the interior details.

SYNC
The relative position in time of one image to another.

T

TABLE–TOP PHOTOGRAPHY
The close–up photography of small objects or sets.

TAILS
The end of a roll of film or videotape.

TAKE
Each filming of a scene from camera start to camera stop is a "take" of that scene.

TAKING CAMERA
A camera which is filming a scene.

TANK SHOT
A special effects shot filmed in a large water tank to simulate a large body of water.

TD/TECHNICAL DIRECTOR
The visual effects crewperson within a COMPUTER GRAPHICS or EFFECTS facility responsible for determining technical approaches to a visual effect and guiding the execution of a project.

TELECINE
A machine which converts film images to video.

TEMP
Abbreviation for TEMPORARY COMPOSITE.

TEMPORARY COMPOSITE
A preliminary version of a COMPOSITE containing all the major ELEMENTS of a shot but which may have visible MATTE lines or incorrect color balance. Except for fidelity of execution, a temporary composite is representative of what the shot will be in terms of any action which might alter the editing of the picture or sound tracts of the film.

TERMINAL
A station, most often remote from the MAINFRAME computer, through which data can be input and retrieved from the computer.

TEST STRIP
See SENSITOMETRIC STRIP.

TEXTURE MAPPING
A process in COMPUTER GRAPHICS in which a surface texture or detail is extracted from one image and applied to another. Applying the texture of the skin of an elephant to an image of a dinosaur is an example.

T GRAIN
A term used by Kodak to describe a new type of silver halide particle in a film EMULSION which is flatter in structure and less visible in the projected image. The new T grain film emulsions produce images with less apparent GRAININESS than older emulsions.

THIRTY–TWO BIT COLOR
Refers to the number of color possibilities for COMPUTER GENERATED IMAGERY when each PIXEL is stored as 32 BITS of information, or roughly 16.7 million colors plus a separate MATTE CHANNEL with 256 available shades of gray. See COLOR DEPTH, EIGHT BIT COLOR, SIXTEEN BIT COLOR, and TWENTY–FOUR BIT COLOR.

35 mm FILM
The standard film gauge for professional filmmaking. 35 mm in width, sixteen frames per foot with four perforations per frame (hence the nickname "four perf".) See FOUR PERF.

3–D
Abbreviation for three dimensional. See STEREOSCOPIC PHOTOGRAPHY.

THREE-D ANIMATION
See STOP MOTION ANIMATION and OBJECT ANIMATION.

THREE-D COMPUTER GRAPHICS
See THREE-DIMENSIONAL COMPUTER GRAPHICS.

THREE-D DIGITIZING
See DIGITIZE.

THREE-D IMAGE
See THREE-DIMENSIONAL IMAGE.

THREE-DIMENSIONAL ANIMATION
See STOP MOTION ANIMATION.

THREE-DIMENSIONAL COMPUTER GRAPHICS
A process of numerically building a three-dimensional character inside a computer and then synthesizing character and camera movements or positions. In this way imaginary scenes are filmed by imaginary cameras.

THREE-DIMENSIONAL DIGITIZING
See DIGITIZE.

THREE-DIMENSIONAL IMAGE
A DIGITAL IMAGE constructed within a computer with all three dimensions of height, width and depth described. Three-dimensional digital images are completely real to the computer and can be rotated or positioned to achieve any desired view of the subject.

THREE-DIMENSIONAL PHOTOGRAPHY
See STEREOSCOPIC PHOTOGRAPHY.

THREE-D PHOTOGRAPHY
See STEREOSCOPIC PHOTOGRAPHY.

THREE PIN MOVEMENT
A camera movement which utilizes three REGISTRATION PINS rather than the more common two pins.

TIME CODE
Sequential numbers in the format of hours, minutes, seconds and frames which designate position on a videotape.

TIME LAPSE CAMERA
A camera which is capable of shooting a single frame of film at regular pre-determined intervals.

TIME LAPSE PHOTOGRAPHY
The process of continuously filming a scene of long duration one frame at a time with relatively long time intervals between frame exposures. The effect of this process is to significantly speed up the action and is used quite often in scientific photography for such images as a flower opening.

TIMING
See COLOR TIMING.

TONDREAU SYSTEM™
A trademarked computer SOFTWARE system designed by Bill Tondreau and widely used as the "brain" of MOTION CONTROL CAMERA systems in special effects photography.

TOUCHSCREEN
A COMPUTER SCREEN which allows the user to select from menu items by touching the surface of the screen either by hand or with a STYLUS.

TRACED MATTE
See ROTOSCOPED MATTE.

TRACKBALL
A device consisting of a semi–encased ball resting on sensors such that when the ball is rolled the sensors are stimulated to move a CURSOR across a COMPUTER SCREEN. A MOUSE is a trackball turned upside down.

TRACK CAMERA
A MOTIONED CONTROLLED camera apparatus generally consisting of a hardened steel track on which a boom unit rides. At the end of the boom is a remote camera pan, tilt and roll mechanism. Track cameras are typically used to photograph miniature sets and models when a good deal of camera movement is required.
(See illustration on page 144.)

TRANSFER
The process of converting an image from one medium to another, such as from film to video.

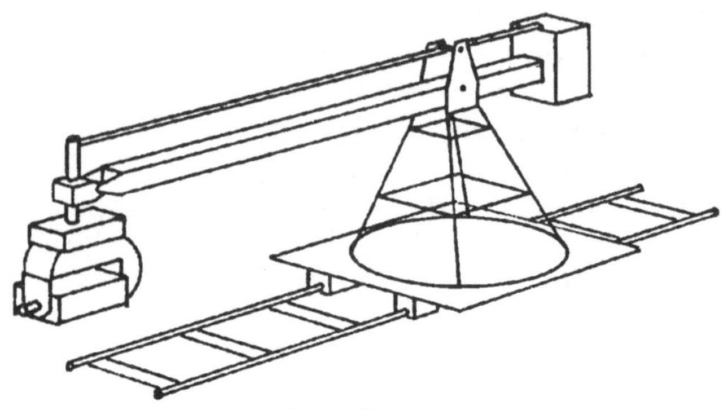

TRACK CAMERA

TRANSFORMATION EFFECT
The effect of changing one object into another. State–of–the–art transformation effects involve the use of COMPUTER IMAGE PROCESSING SOFTWARE. See MORPHING.

TRANSLITE SCREEN
See TRANSLIGHT SCREEN.

TRANSLIGHT SCREEN
A very large translucent photograph used to extend a PRACTICAL set without construction. Translight screens are positioned in the set and lit from behind.

TRANSMISSION BLUESCREEN
A type of BLUESCREEN made of a sheet of translucent and flexible blue plastic, usually a "STEWART T–MATTE™," which is stretched between a rigid frame and lit from behind.

TRANSPARENCY
1) A condition caused by MATTES of insufficient density in which a BACKGROUND image is partially visible through a foreground image.
2) A translucent film image such as a slide.

TRAVELING MATTE
A MATTE which follows the silhouette of a subject as it moves through frame. By conforming to the exact shape and position of the subject for each frame of film, the matte is said to "travel."

TRAVELING MATTE PROCESS
See TRAVELING MATTE, BLUESCREEN PROCESS and SODIUM VAPOR TRAVELING MATTE PROCESS, COLOR

DIFFERENCE MATTING, DIFFERENCE MATTING and COLOR DIFFERENCE TRAVELING MATTE PROCESS.

TRAVELING SPLIT SCREEN
A SPLIT SCREEN shot in which the split line between two segments moves through the frame as the action requires.

TUNGSTEN BALANCED FILM
Color film stock which is chemically balanced to reproduce accurate colors when exposed to tungsten light sources. See COLOR TEMPERATURE.

TWENTY–FOUR BIT COLOR
Refers to the number of color possibilities for COMPUTER GENERATED IMAGERY when each PIXEL is stored as 24 BITS of information, or roughly 16.7 million colors. See COLOR DEPTH, EIGHT BIT COLOR, SIXTEEN BIT COLOR and THIRTY–TWO BIT COLOR.

TWO–D IMAGE/2–D IMAGE
See TWO-DIMENSIONAL IMAGE.

TWO-DIMENSIONAL IMAGE
A DIGITAL IMAGE within a computer which has only height and width defined, and not depth. Two-dimensional images are generally input into a computer by scanning flat artwork or film images. Since a two-dimensional image is flat, computer manipulation of the image is severely limited compared with the power to manipulate a THREE-DIMENSIONAL IMAGE.

ULTRASONIC CLEANER
A film cleaner which uses ultra–high frequency sound waves to remove dirt.

UNDERCRANK
To film at speeds less than normal sound speed of 24 frames per second in order to speed up the action when projected at 24 frames per second.

UNDERDEVELOPMENT
The reduction of the normal processing time allotted for a film EMULSION in order to compensate for overexposure of the negative. Also called PULLING.

UNDEREXPOSE
To EXPOSE a film EMULSION for less than the standard length of time such that the filmed scene appears darker than normal.

UNEXPOSED
A film EMULSION which has not yet been exposed to light is said to be "unexposed."

UNSTEADY
A camera or projector movement or film image which is not steady. See STEADY.

UNSTEADY PLATE
A BACKGROUND scene which was filmed with an unsteady camera. See STEADY and STEADINESS.

VALUE
Also called LIGHT VALUE, the degree of lightness or darkness of an image independent of its color.

VARIABLE SHUTTER
A camera shutter with an adjustable open angle. Variable shutters offer control of the exposure time of each frame, thereby increasing or decreasing the amount of motion blur. See SHUTTER ANGLE.

VASELINE FILTER
A diffusion filter made by smearing petroleum jelly on a piece of glass.

VECTOR GRAPHICS
See COMPUTER GRAPHICS.

VEILING
The undesirable contamination of an image caused by low levels of diffuse light reflecting off the internal glass elements of a lens.

VIDEO DIGITIZER
A device which uses a video camera and a beam of laser light to convert a three dimensional object into an array of numbers which a computer then uses to create a DIGITAL IMAGE of the subject. See DIGITIZE.

VIDEO DISC
See OPTICAL DISC.

VIDEOMATIC
A rough approximation of a scene which is filmed on video tape and often transferred to film for inclusion in an edited sequence. Videomatics are an inexpensive way to accurately establish the speed, timing and composition of an action shot before it is actually photographed. See also ANIMATIC.

VIDEO PAINTBOX SYSTEM
See PAINT SYSTEM.

VIDEO RESOLUTION
The resolution of a video image as measured by the number of horizontal scan lines. Standard video resolution in the United States is 525 lines.

VIGNETTING
Encroachment into the edges of frame of an object in front of the lens.

VIRTUAL IMAGE
An image which can be seen with the naked eye, such as that on a movie screen or a viewfinder.

VISTACRUISER™
A modern MOTION CONTROL TRACK CAMERA built by Industrial Light and Magic company.

VISTAFLEX™
A reflex viewing Vistavision production camera built by Industrial Light and Magic company.

VISTAGLIDE™
A real time MOTION CONTROL dolly and camera gear head built by Industrial Light and Magic company.

VISTAVISION
A film format which uses standard 35 mm film running horizontally through the camera rather than the normal vertical direction. Vistavision exposes an image area twice the size of the standard 35 mm frame, the width of the image being equivalent to eight perforations, hence the nickname "eight perf." See FORMAT.

VISUAL EFFECTS
See SPECIAL VISUAL EFFECTS.

WARM
A term used to describe an image which is too orange, or on the "warm" side of the color spectrum.

WARPING
See IMAGE WARPING.

WAVE MACHINE
A wedge shaped box which is repeatedly dipped into a water tank to create waves.

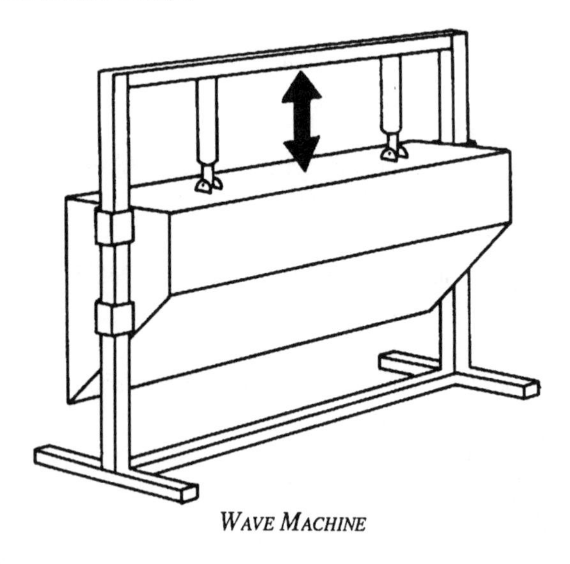

WAVE MACHINE

WEDGE
See EXPOSURE WEDGE.

WEST
A term borrowed from the compass rose which refers to the left hand side of an image or frame.

WET GATE PRINTING
A special process in which a scratched piece of negative is printed while traveling through a gate filled with liquid. The liquid fills the scratch in the negative and prevents light from refraction off the edges of the damage. This printing process renders invisible most scratches which have not actually removed the film EMULSION.

WHITE LIGHT
Light which has no color in and of itself and therefore all objects within such light appear to be their natural colors.

WINDOW
An area within a COMPUTER SCREEN which displays a portion of an image or document. There may be several active windows in order to view different sections of the same file at once.

WIPE
A transitional effect between scenes in which one image seems to replace the other in a sweeping "wipe" across the frame.

WIPE MATTE
See REVEAL MATTE.

WIPE OFF
An image which disappears with a WIPE effect is said to "wipe off."

WIPE OFF ANIMATION
See REVEAL MATTE.

WIPE ON
An image which appears with a WIPE effect is said to "wipe on."

WIPE ON ANIMATION
See REVEAL MATTE.

WIREFRAME ANIMATION
The process of designing the movement of a computer generated image using a WIREFRAME MODEL.

WIREFRAME MODEL
A computer generated model which approximates the contours of a subject by linking KEY POINTS on the surface of the subject with straight lines.

Wireframe Model

WIREFRAME MODEL of the stained glass man from Young Sherlock Holmes. See illustration for DIGITIZING PEN to see how this model was input into the computer. Photo courtesy Lucasfilm Ltd.

WIREFRAME OBJECT
See WIREFRAME MODEL.

WIRE MODEL
See WIREFRAME MODEL.

WIRE REMOVAL
The process of removing visible wires from a scene with the help of a computer.

WIREWORK
The practice of suspending actors on thin wires to simulate flying or levitation such as was done for the example below from "Willow."
(See illustration on page 151.)

WIREWORK

WIREWORK often involves suspending actors, in this case a fairy from "Willow." Photo courtesy Lucasfilm Ltd.

WITNESS MARKS
Marks placed in a scene which serve as position reference for matched move plotting. Also the scribe marks on a lens which serve as the position reference for focus distance and APERTURE settings.

WORKPRINT
The first and/or subsequent copies of all DAILIES of a film which the editor will use while editing the film.

WORKSTATION
A remote device consisting of a KEYBOARD, a COMPUTER SCREEN and other possible PERIPHERAL DEVICES which can be used to input and retrieve information from a computer.

WRAP
To complete a project is to "wrap" it up.

X
A shorthand notation for a single frame.

Z

ZOPTIC FRONT PROJECTION SYSTEM™
A front projection system which utilizes matching motorized zoom lenses on the projector and camera to simulate movement of the subject through frame. The Zoptic system was first made famous during its use on the first "Superman" movie.

INDEX

Terms Relating to Bluescreen and Opticals

Optical Effects
Optical Effects Animation
Optical Flip
Optical Flop
Optical House
Optical Layout
Optical Lineup
Optical Move
Optical Printer
Optical Printing
Optical Reduction
Optical Zoom
Opticals
Optics

P

Paddle
Pass
Pass Through Effect
Pin Registered Optical Printer
Plate
Pre Comp
Pre Composite
Print Through
Printback
Printer
Pull a Matte

R

Reciprocity Failure
Red Record
Reduction
Reduction Only
Reduction Only Composite
Reduction Print
Reduction Rolls
Registered Print
Repo
Reposition
Reverse Action (Printing)
Reverse Bluescreen Process
Reverse Motion
Reverse Printing
Ripple Effect
Ripple Glass
Rock And Roll
Rod Articulate Matte
Roto Matte
Rotoscoped Matte
Rough Comp
Rough Composite

S

Second Generation Dupe
Sensitometer
Sensitometric Strip
Sensitometry
Separation Masters
Separation Positives
Seps
Skip Frame Printing
Skip Framing
Skip Out
Skip Printing
Slip The Sync
Sodium Process
Sodium Vapor Traveling Matte Process
Soft-Edged Matte
Sonic Cleaner
Spill Light
Spill Matte
Split Screen
Split Screen Effect
Step Print
Step Printer
Stewart Traveling Matte
Stewart T-Matte
Streak Pass

T

Temp
Temporary Composite
Timing
Traced Matte
Transmission Bluescreen
Transparency
Traveling Matte
Traveling Matte Process
Traveling Split Screen

U

Ultrasonic Cleaner

W

Wet Gate Printing
Wipe
Wipe Matte
Wipe Off
Wipe On

Terms Relating To Computer Graphics

A

Abekas
Address
Algorithm
Aliasing
Alpha Channel
Alphanumeric
Analog
Animated On Ones/Twos
Antialiasing
Application
Architecture
Artifact
ASCII
Attribute
Auxiliary Storage

B

Baud Rate
Binary
Binary Digit
Bit
Boot
Buffer
Bug
Bus
Byte
B-Spline

C

Cathode Ray Tube
CCD
CCD Array
CD-Rom
Central Processing Unit
CGI
Channel
Charged Coupled Device
Chip
Circuit Board
Color Depth
Color Map
Color Table
Color Test
Command
Computer Assisted Animation
Computer Chip
Computer Controlled Animation
Computer File
Computer Generated Animation
Computer Generated Imagery
Computer Graphics
Computer Interpolation
Computer Screen
Crash
Crosshair Digitizer
CRT
Cursor

D

Data
Database
Debugging
Deformation
Depth Cueing
Difference Matting
Digital
Digital Animation
Digital Composite
Digital Image
Digital Printer
Digitize
Digitizing Pen
Digitizing Scanner
Digitizing Table/Tablet
Diskette
Display
Download
Drop Out
Dynamic Range

E

Edge Detection
Eight Bit Color
Eikonix

Paintbox
Palette
Peripheral Devices
Photoshop
Picture Element
Pixel
Pixel Manipulation
Polygon
Polygonal Modeling
Puck
Pulldown Menu

R

Raster
Raster Display
Raster Graphics
Ray Tracing
Real Time
Reflection Mapping
Removable Hard Disc
Rendering
Rendering An Image
Resizing
Resolution
Rubber Stamp

S

Sample
Scaling
Scan In
Scan Out
Shading
Sharpening Filter
Sixteen Bit Color
Soft Copy
Software
Solitaire
Splines
Squash
Stairstepping
Still Store
Stretch
Stylus
Surface Rendering

T

Technical Director
TD
Terminal
Texture Mapping
Thirty-Two Bit Color
Three D Animation
Three D Computer Graphics
Three D Digitizing
Three D Image
Three D Photography
Three Dimensional Animation
Three Dimensional Computer Graphics
Three Dimensional Digitizing
Touchscreen
Trackball
Transformation Effect
Twenty-Four Bit Color
Two Dimensional Image
Two-D Image

V

Vector Graphics
Video Digitizer

W

Warping
Window
Wire Model
Wire Removal
Wireframe Animation
Wireframe Model
Wireframe Object
Witness Marks
Workstation

Index of Illustrations & Photographs*

*Listings in *italics* are photographs.

About the Author

Micheal McAlister is recognized as one of the industry's top Visual Effects Supervisors. During his tenure of eleven years at Lucasfilm's Industrial Light and Magic he garnered an Academy Award, an Emmy, a British Academy Award, a second Academy Award nomination and a second British Academy Award nomination.

His work has been the subject of many television reports including *Entertainment Tonight, The Today Show, Nova* and various documentary specials both in the United States and abroad. Interviews with Micheal have appeared numerous times in the Industry journals *American Cinematography and Cinefex* .

Micheal is currently in pursuit of a directing career in Hollywood.